Postmodern Theory and *Blade Runner*

FILM THEORY IN PRACTICE

Series Editor: Todd McGowan

FILM THEORY IN PRACTICE

Postmodern Theory and *Blade Runner*

MATTHEW FLISFEDER

BLOOMSBURY ACADEMIC
LONDON • NEW YORK • OXFORD • NEW DELHI • SYDNEY

BLOOMSBURY ACADEMIC
Bloomsbury Publishing Plc
50 Bedford Square, London, WC1B 3DP, UK
1385 Broadway, New York, NY 10018, USA
29 Earlsfort Terrace, Dublin 2, Ireland

BLOOMSBURY, BLOOMSBURY ACADEMIC and the Diana logo
are trademarks of Bloomsbury Publishing Plc

First published 2017
Reprinted 2018, 2021

Cover design: Alice Marwick
Cover image © Shutterstock (Top) / still from BLADE RUNNER (1982) ©
LADD COMPANY / WARNER BROS / THE KOBAL COLLECTION (Bottom)

A catalogue record for this book is available from the British Library.

Library of Congress Cataloging-in-Publication Data
Names: Flisfeder, Matthew, 1980-author.
Title: Postmodern theory and Blade runner / Matthew Flisfeder.
Description: New York: Bloomsbury Academic, 2017. |
Series: Film theory in practice | Includes bibliographical references and index.
Identifiers: LCCN 2016043966 (print) | LCCN 2017006535 (ebook) |
ISBN 9781501311802 (hardback: alk.paper) |
ISBN 9781501311796 (pbk.: alk.paper) | ISBN 9781501311765 (ePDF) |
ISBN 9781501311772 (ePUB)
Subjects: LCSH: Blade runner (Motion picture) | Postmodernism.
Classification: LCC PN1997.B596 F55 2017 (print) |
LCC PN1997.B596 (ebook) | DDC791.45/72–dc23
LC record available at https://lccn.loc.gov/201604396

ISBN: HB: 978-1-5013-1180-2
PB: 978-1-5013-1179-6
ePDF: 978-1-5013-1176-5
eBook: 978-1-5013-1177-2

Series: Film Theory in Practice

Typeset by Newgen Knowledge Works Pvt Ltd., Chennai, India

To find out more about our authors and books visit
www.bloomsbury.com and sign up for our newsletters.

For
Lilah and Zane,
My two little replicants

CONTENTS

ACKNOWLEDGMENTS

Many thanks to Todd McGowan for his guidance, patience, and encouragement in preparing this manuscript.

I am grateful for the friendship and camaraderie shown to me by Louis-Paul Willis and Clint Burnham, who have provided me with insightful feedback on my work.

Colin Mooers, Stuart Murray, and Scott Forsyth continue to be exceptional mentors and I am humbled by their generosity.

Thank you to many other friends, family, and colleagues who have supported me and my work over the last few years: Miriam Anderson, Nicole Cohen, Todd Dufresne, Avrum and Janice Flisfeder, Rochelle Freedland, Antonio Garcia, Agon Hamza, Jason Hannan, Penelope Ironstone, Aleksandra Kaminska, Janine Marchessault, Bob Marshall, Jaqueline McLeod Rogers, Tanner Mirrlees, Andy Mlinarski, Paul Moore, Daniel Paré, Sorpong Peou, Russell Sbriglia, Alan Sears, Imre Szeman, Neil Thomlinson, Adam Thorn, Cindy Zeiher, Joe Zboralski, and Slavoj Žižek.

Nothing I do would be possible without the love, support, and patience of my wife, Robyn Flisfeder, who is uniquely capable of challenging me and keeping me motivated.

Introduction

The term "postmodernism" expresses something quite *peculiar about*, but also something that is rather *particular to* the financial stage of capitalism. In a sense, finance helps to obliterate the future. Finance forces us into an experience of a "perpetual present,"[1] where (out of necessity) we are constantly in the position of borrowing *from ourselves*—from our potential future earnings—so that we can afford our lives in the present. Postmodernism, in this sense, overlaps effectively with consumer society in the form of credit, or the credit card. We experience our lives as a "perpetual present" because we are always working toward catching up with our debts. This is in contrast to the modern ethic of saving and producing, which allowed us to envision some kind of more idealistic future; today, we live in a perpetual present that makes us increasingly cynical of the very possibility of a better world.[2] This is a feature that ties finance to the culture of postmodernism, the evisceration of history, and the "spatialization" of time, overlapping with the culture of the digital and instant access.

Take contemporary online video streaming services like Netflix, for instance. With the streaming of films and TV shows online, it is almost as if there is no longer any beginning or end to the program, just a constant flow or stream of content. YouTube is exemplary of this as well, where it almost feels like we can never stop clicking on the next video; and with social media, too, like Facebook and Twitter, we are barraged by a continuous cascade of torrents. This is, of course, not too dissimilar to the early days of MTV, a channel that was said to exemplify postmodernism precisely because it had no fixed programming, no structured allotment of time; it had only a constant stream of music videos, or what are in effect three-to-five minute commercials for records; certainly, the latter is also a sign of the breakdown between art and commodity in postmodern culture. What we get with this apparently limitless flow of content is just a blanket of information without beginning or end: there is no past and there is no conceivable future. This is the context in which we can come to understand postmodern theory.

To be more precise, postmodernism is a theory of culture comprising of five elements: (1) it approaches culture and history through a critique of metanarratives such as Marxism and psychoanalysis; (2) it focuses on cultural representations in and across media; (3) its attention to new media draws out some of the complications of our experiences of reality; (4) it challenges traditional conceptions of subjectivity and identity, particularly those that tie human identity and human nature to the body and to *self*-consciousness; and (5) it emphasizes pluralism in terms of race, gender, sexuality, and class. With its attention to pluralism, postmodern theory works to dissolve the boundary between high art and popular culture. Instead of seeing popular culture as simply a tool for the reproduction of dominant ideology, postmodernism maintains a pluralistic focus in suggesting that popular culture should be taken seriously as a matter of legitimate cultural expression and pleasure. It shifts attention away from the elite spaces of the gallery and the museum, and moves it into the movie theatre and the shopping mall. However, this makes it especially difficult to discern the *political* in postmodernism, a point that requires some initial elaboration.

Because postmodernism is drawn out by the convergence of culture and commodification, it may be difficult to understand its political orientation or commitments. It accepts the legitimacy of popular culture and the pleasure it provides for its audiences as worthy objects of contemplation, a fact that distinguishes it from the elitism of modern cultural theory and criticism; but by doing so, postmodernism disavows the commodity–class dynamic of capitalism. Therefore, postmodernism can be seen as supportive of the popular classes, but it can also be seen as underserving this population by ignoring the underlying class politics of capitalist society. It is on this topic that much of the debate surrounding postmodernism has developed, especially in its approach to historical metanarratives.

The postmodern critique of metanarratives, I argue, is problematic because it limits our ability to consider political questions in their historical context. Postmodernism does not negate history entirely, but there *is* a tendency in postmodern theory to attend to questions of space instead of questions relating to time and goal-oriented history (or *teleology*), especially theories about historical *progress*. By emphasizing space over time, postmodernism eschews concerns with depth and essence, and prefers to focus on surfaces and appearances. Through its critique of the media, postmodern theory suggests that our experiences of reality are always *preceded* by models and representations, implying, therefore, that our experiences of reality are all a matter of appearance, simulation, and simulacra (or, a copy without an original). There is for postmodernism, in other words, no deeper (single or essential) reality behind the representation; all of reality is a mere matter of mediated simulation. With a focus on issues of representation and surfaces, postmodern cultural objects and texts often comprise references to the past and are filled with quotations of past cultural styles and stereotypes. However, these are references to a *simulated* past, or simulations of cultural stereotypes from the past. This is one of the reasons why history figures into debates about postmodernism, and disputes persist as to whether these references are intended to be ironic, or if they result in the depoliticization of the past (and, consequentially, the present).

Some theorists of postmodernism argue that parody and irony are used in postmodern texts to reference and criticize the past, and in this way, postmodernism is highly political; others suggest that postmodern representations cite historical references to the past, but without acknowledging their source, a practice called pastiche. In doing so, postmodern-ism *removes* the social and political *context* of the cultural object; however, those who claim this last position also pro-pose that postmodernism only reproduces images and refer-ences to the past without reference because it is no longer possible to come up with anything wholly new in culture. It's all been done, so to speak, and, in this way, postmodern culture expresses an "end of history," one of its primary ideo-logical claims.

Ideologically, postmodernism differs from previous concep-tions of power. Today, people follow the dominant ideology, not so much because the truth is hidden—what an older theory of ideology referred to as "false consciousness," but because the truth of the world is in plain sight: we have deep problems with inequality, racism, sexism, and homophobia, for instance; we continue to experience the ramifications of big financial crises, extending the austerity logic of divestment from social and public services; and there are the looming ecological catas-trophes threatening our very existence on Earth. Surely other avowed social, political, economic, and environmental prob-lems persist. However, even though all of these problems are acknowledged, there is a tendency to respond to them cyni-cally, as if there is no other alternative to the current organi-zation of society. "End of history" means that not only is the "new" no longer possible at the level of style, genre, and so on, in cultural objects and texts, but also that no other alter-native to the current system is conceivable. Postmodernism is ideological in *this* way, and in part this ideological condition is given structure by postmodern approaches to history; or, more accurately, postmodern ideology is the product of a negation of a *specific approach* to history: the Marxist conception of historical materialism.

While I value postmodern approaches to the criticism of culture—particularly the postmodern valorization of popu-lar culture, its emphasis on pluralism, and its critique of the Eurocentrism and phallocentrism of modern criticism—the view I espouse in this book is that the political success of post-modern theory is possible only if it is articulated in conjunction with a focus on the commodity and class dynamics of capitalism. That is to say, postmodernism has certainly raised important questions about media and new media, about genre and style in cultural objects and texts, about subjectivity and identity, and issues of race, gender, and sexuality. However, the questions that it raises cannot be fully addressed without considering their relationship to the dynamics of a capitalist society, and the historical transformations brought forth by the latter's development.

By taking a popular film like Ridley Scott's *Blade Runner* seriously—that is, as a serious and legitimate object of contemplation—I will show how it provides a deeper criticism and understanding of the contemporary social, political, and cultural significance of postmodernism and postmodern theory. This book is therefore meant to introduce readers to postmodern theory and criticism through a postmodern analysis of *Blade Runner*; but the analysis of *Blade Runner* will also allow us to better understand our own social, cultural, and political context in twenty-first-century capitalist society. This is an approach that the literary scholar Fredric Jameson—one of the key theorists of postmodernism—discussed in the pages that follow, refers to as "cognitive mapping."[3] Since the postmodern critique of metanarratives problematizes the subject's understanding of herself in time and space, cognitive mapping is an attempt to return her to some type of meaningful, yet politically soluble position. I use popular culture, and *Blade Runner* specifically in this instance, to develop a cognitive map of postmodernism, postmodern theory, and, in the end, the contemporary cultural, social, and political context of postmodern capitalism. By looking at postmodernism in this way, my approach draws largely upon the Marxist tradition for its insights, and especially its materialist understanding of history. We will need, then, to begin with a historical sketch of the emergence of postmodernism and postmodern theory.

Postmodernism and history

Much of the debate about postmodernism concerns the status of history in postmodern theory. Postmodern theory takes its point of departure from modern conceptions of history, particularly those found in political liberalism and Marxism. Liberal and Marxist theories of history are similar in perceiving it as both teleological and as having an origin. In the liberal narrative, there is an original "state of nature" that precedes modern civilization, and history is the movement away from the former and toward the latter. Liberalism is rife with contradictions though, since it often relies upon ideologies of nature to justify its own conception of civilization. Market competition in a capitalist society, for instance, is deemed just since it relies on our natural instincts to act competitively. Liberalism draws upon Enlightenment principles such as freedom, equality, and progress. It aims toward the development of an equal society at the formal level of the law ("equality before the eyes of the law"), but has been unable to understand the limits placed on equality by the necessity for exploitation found in the capitalist mode of production, which is the source of capitalist surplus value or profit.

Marxism, which is also the product of Enlightenment principles, sees history, in contrast to liberalism, from two different lenses that are mutually constitutive. History is understood as the historical transition from one economic basis (or mode of production) to the next—for instance, from a feudal society to a capitalist society; but history is also a record of class struggles. These two lenses intersect since, for Marx, the transition from one mode of production to the next is the outcome of the class struggle. The side of victory in the class struggle is determinative of the mode of production that emerges, develops, or survives, and then becomes the foundation for the development of those political and social institutions that help to support its existence, such as the state, education, organized religion, and the media. Marxism therefore finds historical origin in the class struggle and in the development of the economic mode of production. History will then find its culmination in the formation of a classless, or communist, society. Marxists call this approach "historical materialism."[4]

Postmodernism finds fault with both of these theories (or narratives) of history, suggesting that they are one-dimensional and limit the scope of historical understanding. Postmodern theorists prefer to avoid these kinds of linear historical narratives, seeing them as too normative and reductive, and claim instead that history is the product of *overlapping* narratives and discourses, theories of knowledge, and various types of social and political relationships and interactions. But three aspects of the politics, technology, and economy of the twentieth century have further propelled the postmodern critique of Marxist history in particular. The first is the political failure of European communism; the second is the shift in capitalist society from Fordist to post-Fordist practices of production; and the third is the rise of consumer society and culture. It is worth looking at this context more closely since it provides the necessary background for understanding the postmodern critique of historical materialism, and conversely, the Marxist critique of postmodernism.

From Fordism to neoliberalism

Perhaps the most recognizable image of Fordism is of assembly line production, but Fordism also espouses the idea of paying workers enough in wages so that they are able to buy the products that they help to produce. In effect, workers also become consumers, and assume a different type of consumer status with the rise of mass production and mass culture, of which the production of the T-Model Ford was a part. By paying workers enough in wages to transform them into consumers, the hope is not only to improve the quality of life of the typical worker, but also to avoid a crisis of overproduction, where products made cannot be sold, and therefore profits are lost.

Post-Fordism, then, has meant a shift away from regulated production on the assembly line to more flexible forms of production, accompanied by fluctuations in wages and salary, job stability, and new information technology meant to offset problems of overproduction. This is the case, for instance, in the model of "just-in-time-production," where products are made only as orders come in. Terms that are synonymous with post-Fordism include "post-industrial society," "information economy" (or "information society"), and "knowledge economy," since the shift has been accompanied by the offshoring of industrial production and increase in the commodification of knowledge and information. Fordism and post-Fordism are terms that also reflect the overall political economy in the post–World War II period. Fordism is often referred to synonymously with the welfare state model, whereas post-Fordism signals a transition away from the welfare state and toward contemporary "neoliberalism."

Neoliberalism is a term that refers to the shift away from the Keynesian welfare state model, a model in which capitalists, following the Great Depression and World War II, agreed to give up on short-term profits in order to assure the longevity of the capitalist economy. This meant, for instance, high levels of taxation on wealthy individuals and corporations, which were reinvested into social and public programs such as health and education. This was also a period in which labor unions held a strong political influence, as workers started receiving higher wages and having more leisure time. In the midst of the economic crisis of the early 1970s, capitalists began to reassert their class interests in demanding the dissolution of the welfare state model. In its place, they advocated for less state involvement in the redistribution of wealth, a reduction in wages and leisure time for workers, increased contract and precarious forms of labor, and a stronger reliance on the market rather than the state as a space for accessing needs.

Neoliberalism has meant shifting the way that people see themselves and their position in society. Rather than seeing ourselves as citizens, neoliberalism advocates that we should all see ourselves as individual entrepreneurs. By pushing for the shift from state to market mechanisms of regulation, neoliberalism can also be seen as a period in which the financial sector begins to dominate the economy, as much of the growth in the economy for the roughly forty-year period between the early 1970s and the end of the first decade of the twenty-first century was made possible through the creation of new financial commodities such as mortgage-backed securities and derivatives on stocks, which were previously illegal. The deregulation of the economy in this way therefore helped to forge a moment in which big multinational firms began to dominate and gain power globally.

An incredulity toward metanarratives; or, the cultural logic of late capitalism

Some postmodern theorists claim that the shift away from industrial production and toward an information and service-based, technology and science–driven economy—the so-called postindustrial society—has meant that knowledge and technology are now the underlying forces of change, rather than the class struggle between capital and labor. The term "postindustrial" is not meant to imply that industrial production has ceased. Rather, it means that industrial production has largely moved from the developed to the developing world, where labor is cheaper, and where regulations may be more relaxed. This has meant that information technology is in higher demand as a means of helping to facilitate the now global organization of production. In place of material industrial production, labor in the developed world is now employed in the service and information sectors. For the French theorist Jean-François Lyotard, this transition is one that provides entry into a postmodern theory of history.

In his book *The Postmodern Condition* (1979), Lyotard argues that the knowledge-based economy proves that technology, rather than the class struggle, is a driving force of history. Lyotard argued that grand narratives, or metanarratives of history, like historical materialism, are no longer valid. Grand narrative, according to him, has lost its credibility due to postwar changes in technology, the rise of neoliberal capitalism and the dissolution of the Keynesian economic model, and the reducing threat of the communist alternative. Lyotard therefore defines postmodernism as an "incredulity towards metanarratives."[5]

However, historical materialism still provides a valid theory for the emergence of postmodernism and postmodern theory. According to Jameson, postmodernism is the "cultural logic of late capitalism." In other words, postmodern theories of culture, society, and politics, like that of Lyotard, are reflective of the changes taking place in the political economy of capitalism in the transition from the welfare state model to the neoliberal and financial models of capitalism. While Lyotard eschews grand narrative in his interpretation of postmodernism, Jameson embraces the Marxist narrative as a way to fully discern the fact that changes in the mode of production have affected culture, art, and theory.

Jameson argues that postmodernism should be seen as a "cultural dominant." It is not the only form of culture—there are residual elements of traditional and modern culture in the midst of postmodern culture. But just as finance capital now dominates all of the other practices of capitalist production (such as agriculture, industry, etc.), postmodernism names the cultural style that now ties together all of the others. It is an ideology and a form of cultural expression reflective, first of the rise of consumer society and culture, and then the rising dominance of finance.

The rise of consumer society and the development of the advanced (financial) stage of capitalism form the important social, cultural, and economic background for understanding Jameson's conception of postmodernism. Postmodernism, we might say, arrives historically at a moment of *total* commodification. That is to say, not when *everything* strictly speaking has become commodity, but when everything is *potentially* commodifiable, diffused into the capitalist logic of production. *Post*modernism is thus an aesthetic and cultural category that pronounces a reaction to and against modern art at the particular historical moment when modern art and culture were finally diffused through commodification and institutionalization.

Modern art arose in part as a reaction to the culture of the bourgeoisie and the capitalist mode of production more generally, and was driven by efforts against commodification. Therefore, postmodernism, we might say, is what emerges when this resistance is no longer possible, that is, when there is nothing that is not commodity from the perspective of capital, including art itself. Institutionally as well, postmodernism emerges at that very moment when modern art—itself a practice of subversion—becomes the *official* art, that is, the art of the gallery, the museum, and the cannon—when subversion *becomes* the dominant ideology. How, in this case, is it possible to subvert what is already seen as "subversive"? Herein, again, lies the political problem with postmodernism. While postmodernism privileges the subversive elements of culture, subversion becomes mass produced.

Postmodernism as the cultural logic of late capitalism is thus brought about by the folding in together of art and commodity, the paradigmatic example of which is surely Andy Warhol's "Campbell's Soup Cans." Here, we find the blending of the commodity (the soup can) as art, and art (Warhol's work) as commodity. It is a condition that presages that awful oxymoronic phrase: "commercial art." But the mass culture of the consumer society allows us to rethink the cultural value of *popular* as opposed to avant-garde art. In contrast to the elitism of an earlier modern cultural criticism, postmodern cultural criticism allows us to take seriously cultural objects intended for mass consumption. It is in this sense that commercial art, in the form of a cultural industry good, like popular cinema, can become an object of critical and cultural inquiry, not simply for the purpose of ideology critique—or, in other words, a style of critique that sees in the mass object something that is only negative and passive, reproductive of the dominant ideology—but also in the interests of discerning popular aesthetic enjoyment. This is why, as we will see, a film like *Blade Runner*, intended for mass consumption, can still be regarded as postmodern *art*.

New subjects of history; or, the death of the subject

One of the more positive features of postmodernism, a feature that I take to be one of its central gains, is its approach to subjectivity and identity. However, this approach must also be understood in its historical context. Postmodernism proposes that our identities are a matter of representation and that ideologies of race, gender, and class, for instance, inform how we identify ourselves and how we are identified by others in society. Identities are socially and culturally produced, and are not inherent to our biology. This last theme is often depicted through postmodern representations of technology. By viewing human subjectivity through the prism of cybernetic and digital technology, postmodernism challenges naturalistic conceptions of identity and the self. Science fiction portrayals of cyborgs and artificial life-forms and intelligence, as well as technologies of simulation such as virtual reality, therefore figure heavily in postmodernism because they help to identify the fluidity of identity and of reality.

Dating the emergence of postmodernism to the rise of the postindustrial society, neoliberalism, the rise of consumer society/culture, and the *failure*, then, of Keynesianism, as I have already done above, we should mention that it was *within* the time and space of the social welfare state itself that we witness the emergence of the postmodern conceptions of identity and subjectivity. We might think of the welfare state period as one of *class compromise* between the bourgeoisie and the proletariat, between capital and labor, at least in the West. This was a compromise that enabled to a certain extent the potential rebuilding of the global capitalist economy following the economic decline of the Great Depression. Following the war, capital seemed to sacrifice short-term profit for the long-term stability of the system. It is, then, in this period of class compromise that we find the rise of new social movements (i.e., non-class based social and political movements), from the civil rights movement in the United States and national post-colonial struggles in the Third World, to second wave feminism, the students' movement, the antiwar movement, and the gay liberation movement. During this period of class compromise, political struggle did not disappear; it simply assumed a different form. In other words, in this moment we find the arrival of new (political, but non-class based) "subjects of history." With the rise of non-class based politics, it appeared as though not the proletariat, but an assortment of other political subjectivities might be at the heart of social and political transformation.

The "subject," in this period, also became a topic of critical inquiry, especially in French philosophical circles, most notably in the work of theorists that will concern us in Chapter One, such as Jacques Lacan, Louis Althusser, and Michel Foucault. In different ways, these theorists conceive the subject as a product of ideology. Althusser, for instance, claimed that ideology *interpellates* individuals as subjects—that is, individuals become subjects of ideology when they find themselves identifying with its version of reality and truth, and its source in powerful interests. For Althusser, ideology is a representation: it represents an imaginary relationship of the subject to her real conditions of existence.[6] As an ideological construct, the identity of the individual subject (or person) came to be seen as a mere fiction. The identity of the individual is conceived as the product of an ideological representation or as a product of *discourse*, which could be taken apart and deconstructed, for instance, along the lines of race, gender, and class. This theory of subjectivity therefore pronounced the "death of the subject." Subject is not a stable category of the individual; it is rather an artificial formation that places the individual into a role prescribed by power. When we identify as subjects, we assume the identity assigned to us by powerful interests. Since "subject," then, is merely a category of ideology—of representation and discourse—then the subject must be an artificial construction. Drawing on this theory of the subject, postmodernism recognizes the instability of social, cultural, and political identities, and seeks to deconstruct their ideological bindings.

The "death of the subject" can therefore be thought of in two different ways. On the one hand, the arrival of new subjects of history (in the new social movements, for instance) displaced the older modern conception of the bourgeois individual ego and its counterpart, the Marxist subject of historical change/transformation, the proletariat. On the other hand, the new theory of the subject makes of it something that never actually existed in the first place, which has been constituted as something that is purely fictitious, serving the interests of power.

Such a decentering of the subject is also noticeable in the first place, at the turn from the nineteenth to the twentieth century, with Sigmund Freud's invention of psychoanalysis and the discovery of the unconscious, which displaced the centrality of the individual ego. We are, today, used to thinking of individual identity in terms of the famous phrase, "I think, therefore I am," (in Latin, *cogito ergo sum*) claimed by the French philosopher René Descartes. But Freud's theory of the unconscious proposed that we are not always fully aware of all of our own thoughts, and that our identities are constituted by thoughts that we are not aware that we possess (hence the term *unconscious*). However, postmodernism considers even psychoanalysis as something of a metanarrative, like historical materialism, and a repressive one at that, an argument that is highlighted by two other French philosophers—Gilles Deleuze and Felix Guattari—in their book *Anti-Oedipus* (1972).

Seeing in Freud an ideal for the (re-)constitution of the patriarchal model of the bourgeois conjugal family, Deleuze and Guattari invent a counter-model—"schizoanalysis"—placing the schizophrenic at the center of their theory of the subject of capitalism, displacing Freud's neurotic. In combination with the emergence of the new social movements and the new subjects of history, Deleuze and Guattari helped to provide a language for the discernment of a non-masculine, non-Western, non-corporeal (even) subject of postmodernism. Combined with feminist theory, this variant of the postmodern subject helped to create new insights into the critical orientations that further placed a dent into some of the older grand narratives of modernity, principally Marxism and psychoanalysis. In part, my writing on postmodernism and *Blade Runner* seeks to revive the relevance of Marxism and psychoanalysis to provide a critique of postmodernism as an ideological formation. But why develop this critique now? What is its contemporary relevance nearly four decades since it was first theorized by Lyotard and Jameson? A postmodern analysis of *Blade Runner*, I claim, is useful for responding to this question.

From postmodernism to capitalist realism

Postmodernism is a theory of culture that has been on the wane for the last decade and a half or so, particularly since the turn of the century—or more specifically, since the September 11, 2001, attacks by the terrorist organization Al-Qaeda on the World Trade Center in New York City, and the Pentagon. It's this last event that arguably marks, truly, the arrival of the new century and the end of the so-called long twentieth century.[7] *Blade Runner*, conversely, is a film that has received several "makeovers" so to speak. Most notable are the 1992 Director's Cut, and the 2007 Final Cut of the film. These dates are significant for rethinking postmodernism.

Blade Runner was first released in 1982, at a time when cultural theorists were first mulling over emerging discussions of the postmodern. The year 1992, a decade later, the year in which the Director's Cut of the film was released, marks the final demise of the Soviet Union and the apparent triumph of global capitalism and liberal democracy. It is in this year that the neoconservative political scientist, Francis Fukuyama, published his book *The End of History and the Last Man*, in which he argues that with the end of the Cold War, the world has finally settled on *the* model for utopia: liberal democracy in politics, and the capitalist "market economy." This was a moment when the cynicism of big modern revolutionary projects like the Marxist project of the global proletarian revolution came out in full force, subsumed by the hegemony of the consumer society and its pleasure ethic.

In consumer society, we are told, there is nothing any longer that prohibits our enjoyment. If modernism, preceding the postmodern, was a period in which we were constantly *prohibited* by (patriarchal) authority and discipline from enjoying, postmodernism is that period in which we are now constantly *obligated* to enjoy, since big authority seems to have disappeared (the paternal authority deconstructed and dismissed, the power of big government supposedly diminished), and there is nothing standing in the way of our pleasures. This ethic was transformed in some ways, I would argue, with the 2007–2008 credit crisis that began with the collapse of the housing bubble and the subprime mortgage crisis in the United States. Since this period, a contradiction exists between the pleasure ethic of the postmodern consumer society, and the new regimes of austerity in North America and Europe that demand self-discipline and control. If postmodernism was one of those forces that helped to drive out big revolutionary projects—those that responded to the inherent contradictions of the political economy of capitalism—or, at least, is a response to the cynicism that saw failure in revolutionary projects in the United States and Europe, marked by the squashing of the May 1968 uprisings in Paris, then our own period, which the critical theorist Mark Fisher calls "capitalist realism," is one that is left with the problem of having to rethink emancipatory possibilities. How did we get here? This question makes postmodernism still an important topic of interest.

Postmodern theory was in vogue through much of the 1980s and 1990s in art, cultural, political, and social theory, and it was definitely showcased heavily in the film theory of this period. But times have certainly changed—the experience of the first decade of the twentieth century, bracketed by the September 11, 2001 attacks, and the market crash and credit crisis of 2007–2008, seem to have erased from prominence in many respects the language of "postmodernism," "postmodernity," and "*the* postmodern."

In his book *Capitalist Realism* (2009), Fisher notes three significant differences between postmodernism and capitalist realism that, for him, mark the need for his own new concept: (1) In the 1980s, when discussions about postmodernism gained prominence, alternatives to capitalism still existed (i.e., really existing Socialism); (2) *Post*modernism still maintained a relationship with modernism; and, finally, (3) An entire generation has passed since the end of the Cold War.[8] For Fisher, "capitalist realism" signals, then, the shift from postmodernism to something new. Capitalist realism denotes an experience of total capitalism, where there *is* (apparently) no outside (or actually existing alternative). The alternatives to capitalism—alternatives to liberalism and the bourgeoisie, even—still seemed to exist in dialectical tension with the postmodern in some form, and even in actuality with the existence of the Soviet Union.

Postmodernism was posited as the new dominant culture, antithetical to the remaining surpluses of modernism and modern culture. We might say that capitalist realism emerges at that moment when postmodernism has finally succeeding in fully subsuming all remaining elements of the modern. Or, put differently, it might be conceived as that which arrives once the dialectical movement of modernism has finally run its course, that is, once the modern project of constant and continued change, the evacuation of the old and the construction of the new ("make it new," the desire for development) has finally succeeded in ridding culture, society, and politics of history. In this instance, postmodernism, which still bore some kind of antithetical position against the dominance of capitalism, has even—we might say—subsumed itself, bringing with it a cultural context in which there is definitely no alternative to capitalism. Hence the term capitalist realism. Though I find much value in the way that Fisher theorizes the present as "capitalist realism," the concept itself still seems to signal something of the centrality of the postmodern. It is postmodernism *to the extreme*. The feeling that there is no alternative to the global culture of capitalism is brought forth by postmodernism. Just as critics of the postmodern saw it as a new extension of late modern culture, I see "capitalist realism" as the final stage of the postmodern—late postmodernism, perhaps. How, then, can *Blade Runner* help us to mediate our own historical context, caught between postmodernism and capitalist realism?

Plan of the book

This book is divided into two chapters. The first chapter provides a detailed explanation of the rise of postmodernism and postmodern theory and criticism, especially in its relationship to modernism and modern criticism. I use the term "postmodern criticism" in the sense that I seek both to show how a postmodernist perspective takes up an analysis of cinema and film, but also to show and develop some of the deficiencies of postmodernism itself, looking at it reflexively from the perspective of "capitalist realism" and contemporary changes to the culture industry with digital media and forms of distribution. The second chapter, then, makes use of postmodern criticism for a critical analysis of *Blade Runner*.

I use an "intertextual" method of analysis for conducting a postmodern reading of *Blade Runner*. A key feature of postmodernism is its chiding of depth—the locating of the underlying (true) meaning of the text. Preferring surfaces, intertextuality approaches the film by seeing it in its relation to other texts and objects so that through this practice meaning, we might say, is *produced*, rather than simply read. Texts are read allegorically, and in relation to each other, in order to identify, not their deeper/true (single) meaning; they are read in this way in order to cognitively map our own setting in capitalist realism. In conclusion, I hope to show how this practice is useful even in showing how postmodern theory brings to the surface something more structural about the culture and the society *in which* we read; so that terms like history, society, and politics are troubled, but are not lost. They need to be rearticulated and rethought for the age of capitalist realism.

Notes

1 See Fredric Jameson, "Postmodernism and Consumer Society," in *The Anti-Aesthetic: Essays on Postmodern Culture*, ed. Hal Foster (New York: New Press, 1998), 137.

2 I make a similar claim in my article "Communism and the End of the World," *PUBLIC* 48 (2013): 105–15.

3 Fredric Jameson, "Postmodernism, or, the Cultural Logic of Late Capitalism." *New Left Review* 146 (1984): 52–93.

4 It is worth noting that this is still a skewed sketch of historical materialism since, in fact, it does not see the arrival of a classless society as inevitable, but as the only real solution to problems of exploitation found in capitalist and precapitalist societies.

5 Jean-François Lyotard, *The Postmodern Condition: A Report on Knowledge*, trans. Geoff Bennington and Brian Massumi (Minneapolis: University of Minnesota Press, 1984), xxiv.

6 Louis Althusser, "Ideology and Ideological State Apparatuses (Notes towards an Investigation)," in *On Ideology*, trans. Ben Brewster (New York: Verso, 2008).

7 See Giovanni Arrighi, *The Long Twentieth Century: Money, Power, and the Origins of Our Times* (New York: Verso, 1994); see also Alain Badiou, *The Century*, trans. Alberto Toscano (Malden, MA: Polity, 2007).

8 Mark Fisher, *Capitalist Realism: Is There No Alternative?* (Winchester, UK: Zero Books, 2009), 7–8.

CHAPTER ONE

Postmodernism and postmodern theory

Toward a theory of the postmodern

My approach to postmodernism involves first providing a historical sketch of its emergence, and especially its relationship to modernism. Since, in my view, postmodernism is on the one hand the product of transformations in the political economy of capitalism, and on the other hand, initially a reaction to the *commodification* and *institutionalization* of modernism, it is necessary to first look at some of the key features of modernism and modern culture. After providing an initial sketch for the historical emergence of postmodernism, I go on to explain its chief characteristics and themes, and some of its methods of analysis, including categories such as pastiche/parody, irony, double-coding, allegory, its conceptions of subjectivity and identity, and the concept of the hyperreal. Bearing all of this in mind, though, my central argument in what follows is that postmodernism has made some significant gains in terms of its critique of the elitism, Eurocentrism, and phallocentrism of modern cultural criticism; its theories of media and new media add to our understanding of ideology and representation; however, by disavowing the historical materialist approach to culture, the radical and political potential of postmodern theory and criticism is effectively lost.

As we have already seen in the introduction, postmodernism is a theory of culture that begins as a critique of historical metanarratives. It draws attention to media representation as constitutive of our experiences of reality, and likewise challenges representations of traditional conceptions of subjectivity and identity. Postmodernism emphasizes a pluralistic approach to culture, breaking down distinctions, not only of class, but of race and gender as well. With its critique of metanarrative, media representation, and the category of the subject, postmodernism challenges distinctions between essence and appearance, depth and surface, authenticity and inauthenticity, and high and low culture. Essence, depth, and authenticity are viewed as markers of power and elitism, which are dependent upon sharp divides between high art and popular culture. Postmodernism, therefore, breaks down the barriers between high and low culture, and prefers to focus on surfaces and appearances, and the subjective experiences of spectators, which are neither authentic nor inauthentic, but seen simply as affective.

Postmodern theory has made some important gains with its critique of modernism. It is evident that postmodernism is an attempt to distance itself politically from some of the more dubious aspects of modernism. Its attention to questions about race and gender, as well as its approach to new media and popular culture, improve upon the failures of modernism. However, while doing so, postmodernism, I claim, has gone too far in seeing historical materialism as overly Eurocentric and phallocentric, and has been too cynical in rejecting its conception of emancipation—a conception that is perhaps one of the merits of modernism. We will need to then consider what is at stake in modernism before moving onto our discussion of postmodernism. It is, after all, referred to as *post*modernism. The "post" of "postmodernism" can be read in different ways. It may be regarded as a historical *period*, and one that proceeds from modernism. But it can also be read as a criticism and negation of modernism.

Although we can say that postmodernism follows modernism historically, we shouldn't be too stringent in claiming any specific historical break between the two. Emergent elements of postmodernism were certainly present in modernism; likewise, residual elements of modernism are present in postmodernism. Postmodernism shares many of the attributes often associated with modernism, a fact that sometimes makes them difficult to distinguish. Postmodernism shares with modernism a rejection of realism and mimesis (or realistic imitation), as well as linearity in narrative forms. However, it challenges modernism's elitist division between high culture and popular or mass culture. At a formal level, modernism sought to distort classical and traditional practices of realistic and natural depictions of the world, though the natural world remained in dialectical tension with modernism as the referent against which it created distance. Modernism, in other words, still required a conception of naturalism and realism in order to make its own formal practices meaningful. Postmodernism, conversely, negates more aggressively the reference to the real or natural world, insofar as one of its primary claims is that the real world (out there) is nonexistent. It does not exist, that is, *until* it is represented. Reality is only partial, never complete. From the perspective of postmodernism, all meaningful reality is but mere representation—there is, in other words, no one "true" meaning in the world; there are instead a plurality of competing discourses producing "truth effects."

There are two ways of explaining the postmodern renunciation of depth, essence, and authenticity: first, it could be argued that the postmodern reliance on simulation makes any reference to some underlying essence or reality fallacious—if everything is now just mere copy or simulacrum (a copy without an original) then the pursuit of some underlying meaning becomes futile. Meaning is simply the process of linking texts together in an intertextual relation of back and forth referencing. A good example might be the animated comedy series *Family Guy* (1999–Present), where all of the jokes mainly rely on references to insider knowledge and the parody of other popular TV shows and movies, from *Star Wars* (1977) to *The Breakfast Club* (1986). But postmodernism also renounces depth for a more politically radical reason—it sees the pursuit of depth, essence, and authenticity as wholly ideological categories that preserve high/low power dynamics. Claims toward some underlying true meaning, from a postmodern perspective, is always somehow saturated with power and ideology. In this vein, postmodernism also tries to do away with the notions of subjectivity and authority that defined modern sensibilities toward the artist or *auteur*. Instead, postmodernism prefers a more "readerly" and pluralistic approach to the text. The reader's interpretation is just as valid as that of the author—and, in fact, according to thinkers like Roland Barthes and Michel Foucault, the *author*, like the subject, is now "dead," meaning that her input matters less than that of the reader.[1] For postmodern theory, then, there is no one true meaning of the text, never a single unified meaning in the text that interpellates the spectator or reader as a subject. There are instead many *subject positions* from which the text may be read, without any one reading being granted more authority or authenticity over another. Postmodern theory is interested, in this sense, with pluralism as opposed to a single identity or totality.

Postmodernism combines elements of high and popular culture, producing new forms populist art. This has had the double effect of bringing high art down to the masses while simultaneously raising mass culture to the level of high art. To understand this, one only has to consider the work of pop artists like Roy Lichtenstein, for instance, who took the mass cultural form of the comic strip to produce tongue-in-cheek parodies of mainstream American culture. Instead of creating or emphasizing strict borders between high and low culture, postmodernism thus attends to the popular and the vernacular, transforming the everyday into art. Embracing the popular, postmodern art is an attempt to negotiate between the anti-consumerist ideals of modernism—with its vocation to not become commodity—and the commodified mass culture of the people. Whereas modernism is defined by novelty, innovation, and originality (i.e., the ethic to "make it new"), postmodernism embraces tradition, quotation, referencing, and borrowing from past styles and local particularities. Postmodernism, significantly, is also a product of modern commercial mass media, where nothing escapes incorporation into the world of commodification and consumerism. The result has been a kind of retrograde practice of innovation—if the "new" has been exhausted by commodification, then all that remains is a simulation and repackaging of the old as *pastiche*. Alternatively, this repackaging has been regarded by some postmodern theorists as a valid form of *political* criticism, which references the past ironically, parodying those aspects of modern culture that it finds contestable.

Postmodern theory is thus an attempt at shunning what it sees as an apparent apolitical stream in modern art. One of the goals of modern art was the attempt to create an autonomous space of cultural production, separate from religious, moral, and political concerns and interests, hence the modern axiom "art for art's sake." Yet this last fact is contradicted by modernism's constant quest toward novelty, innovation, and the breaking of formal boundaries. The modern quest to "make it new" makes modernism *inherently* political. Although it appeared to exist as a (relatively) autonomous sphere of cultural production separate from that of the political and the economic, by positing the very boundaries that it sought to break modernism identified a political and cultural antagonism. It was a politics *in disguise*, therefore concealing the actual subjective position from which it spoke. Postmodernism chides the ardent formalism of modern art and art criticism, and seeks instead to read and interpret art and culture across texts, methods, and media (i.e., intertextuality). Therefore, one of the positive features of postmodernism, a reaction to modern criticism, is its attempt to dissolve the "critical distance" between art, culture, and the political.

Postmodernism is much more self-reflexive about its stake in the sphere of the political. It is political in a way that is similar to modern art, but in a much more direct and pronounced manner. Its politics are overt, claiming to locate art and representation precisely in its political context, highlighting its underlying normative assumptions—assumptions that position it within the authoritative framework of the West, the masculine, and the elite. Somewhat paradoxically, though, while both modernism and postmodernism are about breaking with (and subverting) authority, postmodernism—as I explain below—occurs when and where subversion of authority becomes increasingly normalized, or, put differently, when modern art, which dealt heavily with breaking boundaries, itself becomes canonized. This last point makes it difficult to conceive the truly radical potentials of postmodernism: How is subversion possible once subversion itself has become the norm?

Consider, for instance, the relationship between "mainstream" culture and subculture. The mainstream consumer culture is fully capable of absorbing and diffusing subculture, which seems contrary and antagonistic to the mainstream, by turning the signs and symbols of the subculture (for example, punk hairstyles, piercings, tattoos, etc.) into commodities for sale on the market.[2] Subculture can also be diffused by incorporating its styles and imagery into popular trends and lifestyles, or by reducing the difference of the subculture to the sameness of the mainstream culture: a punk birthday party, for instance. Think of recent advertisements for KIA cars, where a group of Goth teenagers finally learn to enjoy the pleasures of racing through the outback. At first they appear averse to such experience, but they swiftly throw away their inhibitions and really learn to enjoy it.

If all resistance can now be accommodated by the mainstream—if resistance, in other words, is now *part* of the mainstream, part of the official culture—what remains of the ability to resist the official culture? It may be argued then that a distinctive feature of postmodernism is its reliance on "double-coding"—in the same gesture postmodern representations must affirm *and* subvert the dominant (modern/commercial) culture. Nevertheless, when resistance itself becomes part of the mainstream, something rather peculiar begins to occur: the conservative Right starts to look increasingly like the only radical alternative to dominant culture—hence we also see the rise of the new Right and neo-conservatism arriving in parallel with the emergence of postmodernism in the 1980s and into the present, itself using images and themes of rebellion to appeal to the masses, making it appear as though the Right is a truly counter-hegemonic force. The tea party movement is, here, exemplary, with its disdain for big government, "political correctness," and affirmative action, which it views as wholly oppressive practices of domination, a sign that a "liberal" big brother is in charge.[3] The politics of postmodernism, I claim, are therefore a decontextualized "politics without politics." Without the necessary historical context and background of postmodern theory and criticism, its politics risk dissolving into commercialism, right-wing populism, or cynical resignation. In fact, a Marxist interpretation of postmodernism allows us to discern in it the parallels that it maintains with the ongoing developments of capitalist society. But in order to see this continuity, we must now turn toward a discussion of modernism.

Modern beginnings

If we think of postmodernism as the product of a new stage in the capitalist mode of production, then it is not too difficult to locate its continuity with modernism, itself the product of a previous stage of capitalism (what V. I. Lenin saw as its imperialist stage). Modernism and modern life were marked on the one hand by excitement, novelty, and a striving toward progress and utopia. There are a great many marvels that come out of the modern period: new scientific discoveries that changed the way we saw and understood the universe, new technologies of modern production and the rise of industry and mass communication, new urban environments that saw the eradication of the decay of the old town, and a newer and faster pace of everyday life. These marvels were met, though, by contradictory forces. Modernism witnessed the rise of corporate power and the deepening of the class struggle, and modern industry and the rise of capitalism in the nineteenth century saw many people displaced and relocated into the shocking atmosphere of the metropolis.

Modernity was tied up in a dialectic of development and destruction, of expansion-demolition-expansion.[4] It is to this experience that the great modern artists of the mid- to late-nineteenth century, and the early twentieth century found themselves responding. They dealt passionately with the new environments, rhythms, technologies, and practices of modernization. Nevertheless, they too, lived in dialectical tension with this environment, finding themselves safely at home within it, seeing in it tremendous possibility, but also witnessing its most alienating effects. It is out of this experience that we find the formation of the various modern formalisms and revolutionary art practices and manifestos, from the Impressionism of Renoir and Manet, to the Cubism of Picasso, Italian Futurism of Marinetti, Van Gogh and Munch's Expressionism, Duchamp and Dadaism, the Surrealism of Dali, and finally the Abstract Expressionism of Pollock.

Dealing with the new experiences of modernity, modern artists turned away from the realism of the past, sparked in part by the development of new practices of verisimilitude from journalism and historiography to the invention of the Daguerreotype. With these new practices, enmeshed in a scientific and positivistic obsession with objectivity, rationalism, and empiricism, modern art found itself striving to find a purity of art. Modern art involved itself in the pursuit of a purely self-referential art object, and for later modern art critics the main concern of art would and should be the art object itself: "art for art's sake." The great destructions of the early twentieth century in World War I and the Russian Revolution, the shock to the sensory brought about by the electrification of the modern cities and their architectural marvels like the skyscraper, and the vast new creative and destructive potentials of modern industry, gave artists reason to turn against the social and even the political, all the while still enacting a form of politics in their own practices of negation.

Modernity as a historical epoch refers roughly to a period that began at the end of the sixteenth and the beginning of the seventeenth centuries—an epoch that started with the European Enlightenment. But not the Enlightenment alone: modernity is the historical epoch in which we see the rise of the capitalist mode of production; an event that read through the prism of Marx and Engels's *Communist Manifesto* allows us to understand historical change and development in a wholly new way. The rapid transformation of the capitalist economy and the rise of the bourgeoisie as a class is historically paralleled with the rapid rise of industrialization, the transformation of new economic centers of commerce in the great modern cities, shifts in the structures of population, and new technological innovations that changed the way we think about a whole range of social and cultural activities, from transportation and communication, to the consumption and experience of art and culture.

Modernity is also a period of a political shift away from the *ancien regimes* of the old European monarchies to the institution of the state and the rule of law, or toward modern democracy. The political and the economic fold into each other in important ways in this period, one consequence of which, with global importance, is the rise of new colonialisms and imperialisms, arising out of necessity as demanded by the capitalist imperative to incorporate the world into the process of production for profit. With modernity, we witness the beginnings of what is now called "globalization," or the total incorporation of all corners of the world into the capitalist system.

Modernism is the name given to the rising field of European and then American art beginning in the mid-nineteenth century, which began to wane in the postwar period—the period where we start to hear about a new postmodern art and culture. Modern culture can largely be understood as the result of a dynamic dialectical relationship between new liberal bourgeois sensibilities and the field of aesthetic production working to *resist* bourgeois culture. The latter, though, still holds a tenacious relationship with the field of culture that resisted it: enlightened bourgeois culture became the very prism of *validation* for the new culture of modernity and modern aesthetics.

Although we might think of modernity as a past historical moment, especially since we are claiming that a full-fledged postmodernity has emerged since the postwar period in Europe and the United States, it is still, according to the German social theorist Jürgen Habermas,[5] an "incomplete project." What remains incomplete for Habermas is the project that began with the European Enlightenment. That is, a project that began with the social, political, and economic transition from feudalism to capitalism. It is a project that began with the political rupture of the French Revolution, and aligns itself with the emergence of the scientific method, conceptions of objectivity and truth, rationality, and progress in a moral and material sense. The project of the Enlightenment, described by the philosopher Immanuel Kant as the movement from "immaturity" to "maturity" or from ignorance to (empirical) knowledge. The project of modernity can be characterized, in this sense, precisely as a transition from the old to the new—thus, cry the moderns:

"Make it new!"

Novelty, in the various spheres of knowledge, from the Enlightenment onward, is the driving ethic, not of *dismissing* completely the old or the past, but of making it the measure against which to evaluate the present. This has been true in particular in the fields of art and culture, technological innovation, and in the rapid development and expansion of the capitalist mode of production. Modernism, in the sphere of culture, tries to grapple with the permanent revolution—the constant push for change and transformation—of modernity. Running parallel to permanent revolutions in the capitalist mode of production, and to the rapid technological developments of the period, "newness" is perhaps the most distinguishing feature of modernism: novelty that rebels against all that is normative. But what happens when transgression of the norm *becomes* the norm? This is a problem that, as we will see, is addressed by postmodernism and its critique.

We need to understand modernity, as well as its lineage back to the European Enlightenment, as a period that developed a growing desire for the "rationalization" of the world—this, for Habermas, is part of its "project." It is precisely the "rationalization" of experiential reality into objective fields of empirical knowledge that frames for modern art, on the one hand, the terrain of its aesthetic evaluation, and, on the other hand, the spirit against which it rapidly and continuously sought to reinvent the "new." Likewise, it is the very rationalization of art—that is, its institutionalization—that helps us later on to understand the shift from modernism to postmodernism. Postmodernism can be read, in a sense, as a reaction to the final, thorough, and complete *institutionalization* of modern art. Postmodernism, we might say, is what happens to art and culture when novelty and transgression become (somewhat counter-intuitively) normalized, legitimized through institutions like the gallery and the university. The institutionalization and (as we will see) the commodification of modern art are thus two points of convergence that bring about the emergence of the postmodern. A first step toward the institutionalization of modern art was its instrumentalization through the breakdown of spheres of knowledge into separate disciplines.

The instrumentalization of knowledge

Habermas explains another distinguishing element of modernity: its separation of the older fields of religion and metaphysics into three autonomous spheres: science, morality, and art. These three separate spheres are the result of the dissolution, brought forth by the Enlightenment, with the older traditional, religious, and metaphysical worldviews. The problems inherited from premodern times could then be translated into new "regimes of validity": truth (science), normative right-ness (morality), and authenticity and beauty (art). From this, it followed that these spheres could be institutionalized into scientific discourse(s), theories of morality and jurisprudence, and the production and criticism of art. As well, each of these spheres came with their own set of experts and intrinsic pro-fessional structures: cognitive-instrumental in the realm of science, moral-practical in the realm of the law, and, aesthetic-expressive in the fields of art and criticism.

Somewhat problematically, this process of instrumental-ization, or rationalization, increasingly produced a *cleavage* between the field and culture of the professional experts and that of the larger population. So, while art criticism developed as an autonomous sphere of knowledge, its objective of cre-ating rational self-knowledge—the move from immaturity to maturity that Kant made prominent in his depiction of the Enlightenment—was kept outside and apart from the everyday life world of the popular classes.

By the mid-nineteenth century, and alongside new devel-opments in technologies of representation (photography and later film), art ceased being about direct representation and verisimilitude (realism), and started focusing on the medium of expression itself as *the* art object. Hence the expression "art for art's sake." So we see, for instance, with Impressionism a movement away from earlier realism, perhaps inspired by the invention of photography in the 1830s, and the ability to technologically reproduce the image—that is, the production of technological verisimilitude. On the one hand, modern art set itself a task of constantly and inevitably transgressing the old and the normative ("Make it new!"); on the other hand, its drive had become tautological, separating it from realm of the everyday, from the social and the political, thus distancing itself from the imperatives of the Enlightenment—particularly the aspect of educating the masses, raising them up from their state of immature ignorance toward enlightened knowledge. In this way, modern art embraced formalism over and above rationalism and enlightenment.

By this time, bourgeois art criticism had set up two expectations: first, that the layperson who came to enjoy art must make it his mission to educate himself and become an expert; second, he must make use of art, and relate it to his own life experiences, so that he is enabled to perceive the world in another new way. How then to deal with the ethic, or imperative of "art for art's sake," while at the same time treating art as an avenue of enlightenment, knowledge, and truth? As we will see, it is this very dialectical relationship between the art world and the real world of the social and political that is, on the one hand, the engine of development for modern art, and on the other hand, the contradiction itself is something that is sublated by the emergence of the postmodern. Postmodernism makes of this contradiction one of its own points of negation— the combination of high and low culture—rejecting the elitism of modern art and criticism.

The commodification of art and the art market[6]

The commodification of art is also a contributing factor for the emergence of modernism, and then later, as this process has reached its apogee, for postmodernism. Reading the emergence of modern culture against the background of modernity, modernization—or the technological shift toward industrialization—and the rise of the capitalist mode of production provides additional insights into the later emergence of postmodernism. Capitalism brought with it new class categories (the bourgeoisie and the proletariat), and perceptions about the world and its direction. Capitalism has also largely resulted in the constant and continued commodification and reification (i.e., the rationalization and "thingification," or objectification) of all aspects of human life. Marx's analysis of capitalism teaches us to see in something like commodification the dialectical tension between its potentially repressive and its potentially emancipatory aspects. If bourgeois culture has been about the development of a liberal enlightened society, it has also been about developing a more compliant, efficient, and instrumental form of organization and relationship between people, all in the interests of pursuing ever greater and expanding profits. With the rise of capitalism, all things are potentially commodifiable—that is, they can be turned into a commodity for sale on the market.

Marx's analysis of the contradictions of the capitalist mode of production begins by looking at the commodification of labor power or a person's ability to work and produce a commodity. In his analysis, Marx shows that capitalist profit (or surplus value) is produced first by transforming the worker's *ability* to work itself into a commodity for sale on the market, which is bought by the capitalist and then put to work, producing more value than what it sells for itself (wages) on the market. The source of surplus value, or profit, in capitalism, according to Marx, originates in this relationship, where workers produce more value for the capitalist than what they receive in wages. However, the source of surplus value in capitalist exploitation of labor is hidden from both the worker *and* the capitalist. This fact is masked by the exchange of money (wages) for labor, creating the *appearance* of a fair and (more importantly) *equal* relationship. This is what Marx referred to as "commodity fetishism." The commodity (i.e., money) helps to make possible capitalist relations of exploitation, while it also hides this fact from both the proletariat *and* the bourgeoisie. Although this analysis focuses mainly on the capitalist relations of production, it is also important to pay attention to the way that commodification operates in the sphere of cultural production and art. Capitalism, bourgeois culture, and the primacy given to the space of the "market" produce a new context, as well as cultural and economic *millieus*, for the production and consumption of art and culture. More significantly, it also produces a new working context for artists—that is, the image of the "starving artist"—and their social and political relationships with patrons and consumers of art.

In a sense, the commodification of art has helped lead toward a "democratization" of art. In the old order of the premodern society, art was privileged only for patrons, the aristocracy, the nobility, and so on. With the commodification of art, it now becomes accessible to everyone *equally*, for a price. The apparent market sense of equality (exchange of wage for labor, money for commodity) returns in this case. We can all experience the beauty and aura, or authenticity, of the work of art in the museum, and a kind of egalitarianism is produced by removing art and culture from the private collection of the patron, and placing it into the public space of the gallery. Nevertheless, the cost of admission demonstrates the dialectical tension in place between equality and commodity. All may enter, so long as they can afford it. It is in this sense that art and culture are only *apparently* democratized under capitalism.

Just as art and culture are democratized in this sense, so too is the artist, now "liberated" in modernity (along with the emergence of a whole array of new middle class professions) from older associations, "freed" to produce for himself and sell his work on the market. This newfound liberation had a tremendous impact on the emergence of modernism. The market became a space for the artist to sell his now commodified labor power—commodified and congealed, still, in the form of his labor *and* the work of art. The market also became a space for the sale of art (the commodification of the artist's work and the work itself come tied together in a single extendable form of objectification—the art object stands for the commodification of both the art and the artist). We should now read the ethic of "art for art's sake" under the prism of the market. "Art for art's sake" speaks to the desire to have a sphere carved out for art and cultural production *separate* from the market.

With the universal commodification of labor power under capitalism, which was the starting point for Marx's analysis of capital, all forms of labor and human activity are equated through the exchange of money. But this creates a problem for art, which is deemed authentic through its uniqueness. The commodification of art, equating it with money, and as a result, with other commodities, therefore devalues the authenticity of art. Furthermore, with the advent of photography, it also became possible to reproduce images of art, making it available to a mass audience, removing its uniqueness in space and time, or its "aura."[7] The mass reproduction of the art object, in this way too, makes it more "democratic," but for some modern art critics its reproducibility degrades something of its value, turning it into mere mass culture.

Think, for instance, of Leonardo da Vinci's *Mona Lisa*, which is fully recognizable by a mass audience, as it is reproduced *ad infinitum* on coffee mugs, kitchen aprons, and computer mouse pads, which have all reduced the authentic experience of the object to a kind of shocking inferiority. Is it not the case that when one goes to see the original painting in the Louvre, one finds the real thing meager in comparison to the countless reproductions one now sees all over?[8] Modern art, therefore, struggled with this contradiction between commodification/democratization, and the attempt to carve out a separate sphere for the valuation of art *from* the market. This fact makes it possible to read modern art in relation to commodified mass culture.

What drives modern art is precisely its *vocation to not be commodity*,[9] which is the form occupied by mass culture (what we might today refer to as "popular culture"). Modern art—so-called high culture—exists in a dialectical tension with commodified mass culture. It might, therefore, seem to make good sense to view high culture as holding a primary position within the dialectical relationship between modern art and mass culture, the latter commodifying the former. However, we can locate the emergence of modern art precisely in its drive and objective to fall outside or away from commodity culture. Mass culture is therefore, retroactively, given priority in the relationship between commodification and art. Modern art is precisely that which develops as the negative correlative of commodified mass culture. Nevertheless, because the market quickly diffuses high culture back into mass culture through commodification (at an ever increasing pace with the progression and development of the capitalist mode of production), there is a constant incentive for high culture to revolutionize, to develop and move beyond the old, to "Make it new!" This is an incentive that was pronounced by the modern avant-garde.

The avant-garde and kitsch

There are two perspectives that I would now like to consider regarding the modern distinction between art and mass culture. Both perspectives are raised because they are exemplary of the kind of elitism present in modernism against which postmodern theory rails. The first comes across in the writings of the twentieth-century American art critic Clement Greenberg, particularly in his essay "The Avant-Garde and Kitsch" (1939).[10] The second, which I discuss below, comes from the work of the Frankfurt School theorists, Theodor Adorno and Max Horkheimer. Both perspectives prioritize high art over and above mass culture. Postmodernism is partially a reaction to this kind of elitism, and seeks to dissolve the distinction between high and low culture, and therefore a discussion of the two perspectives that follow help us to understand the terms in which postmodernism was to later assert its own pluralistic approach to culture.

Greenberg's writing on the "avant-garde" is equally important because of the way he identifies a paradoxical relationship between modern art and the bourgeois culture. Modern art was a product of bourgeois society, but was also constantly trying to distance itself from it. According to Greenberg, the "avant-garde" was made possible as part of Western bourgeois society by a new cultural sensibility toward history, and its birth coincided with the scientific revolution of the European Enlightenment. The historical criticism that emerged out of bourgeois culture considered the relationship between past and present in terms of cause and effect. This was a type of historical consciousness, he says, that was then absorbed by artists and poets in the late nineteenth century. Basing their own consciousness (or conscientiousness) upon the bourgeois sentiments about modern history, as opposed to the ancients, modern artists defined *themselves* against a conception of the "bourgeoisie." The Bohemians, in particular, set themselves up *against* the concept of the bourgeoisie to show *what they were not*—that is, they sought to distance themselves from the markets of capitalism, into which, as we have seen, artists had been absorbed as part of the dissolution of aristocratic patronage. It is not too difficult to see here the literary images of the so-called starving artist or writer. Nevertheless, it was not as if the modern artist could rupture completely from the bourgeoisie, the latter still playing the role of patronage.

By separating itself from society, the avant-garde repudiated *both* the bourgeoisie *and* revolutionary politics. Modern art made no allegiances to either side of the class conflict—even though at a material level, there is far more evidence to suggest that the artist was of a proletarian class position due to his position in the relations of production. Baz Luhrman's *Moulin Rouge* (2001) is "typical" in its realization of this scenario. Christian, the poor writer, is interested only in expressions of love. He sees in his writing—his art—an avenue for expression of love and is caught in the romantic Bohemian obsession with "art for art's sake," separated off from the political realm of the class struggle. Despite the clear class conflict that exists between him and the duke—the patron of the troop's "modern" musical *Spectacular Spectacular*—the film sticks to the depoliticized theme of love (developed quite exquisitely in a particularly postmodern pastiche of contemporary pop songs about love). Though echoing the social class conflict, the Bohemian here is removed from the political conflict at the heart of society, freed from the class determination of both the artist and his art. The goal of the avant-garde artist then became one of raising his or her art to the level of *the* absolute; and, ridding itself of (or resolving) contradictions become beside the point; hence the tautological justification of modern art, once again, of "art for art's sake."

For the avant-garde artist, the value for which he is in search of the absolute is the value of the aesthetic, and so he turns toward the processes of imitation in art itself, turning away from subject matter "in common," or popular experience that is, the experience of the masses. By doing so, the artist reacts to the medium. This move provided the very turn toward *the abstract* in modern art, which had become *the imitation of imitation*. Nonrepresentational or abstract art stems from its relationship to some original reference point. With modern art, the constraint of being tied to some original, common world of experience is renounced. Instead, it is the very *processes* of art and writing themselves that become the subject matter of modern art. It is in this sense that modern art became the imitation of imitation, and it is here too that we can locate modernism's obsession with pure formalism.

Just as the avant-garde artists sought to distance themselves from the market, so too, according to Greenberg, did the bourgeois audiences for modern art begin to move away from the avant-garde. The dwindling of the avant-garde and its audience was a sign of the emerging threats to art and culture brought on by mass culture and "kitsch," or popular, commercial art. Kitsch is the result of industrialization, urbanization, and universal literacy. The new urban proletariat and petit bourgeoisie became literate for the sake of efficiency in work and city living, but they still did not possess the leisure time and accessibility necessary for enjoying art and culture. Though, having moved into the cities in pursuit of work, the new urban working class had lost a sense of taste for their older folk cultures, and had become alienated and bored in city living. According to Greenberg, this sense of boredom on the part of the urban proletariat placed pressure on society to provide new forms of amusement; and in order to meet this new demand, a new commodity arrived on the market—mass culture.

These shifting relationships between the avant-garde and the wider public are a further demonstration of the dialectical tension at the heart of modernism: first, modern artists distanced themselves from the bourgeoisie—upon which it was in fact dependent as a financial lifeline; second, the bourgeoisie distanced itself from the avant-garde culture and modern art; third, the new arrival of the *literate* urban working class created a demand for a culture of amusement; and finally, the new conditions of urban commodified mass culture, upon which rose the industrial wealth of the bourgeoisie, became the primary point against which modern art sought to distance itself. Kitsch welcomes and cultivates insensibilities toward genuine culture since it helps to secure profits. It is marked by "faked" sensations. Whereas modern art imitates the *processes* of art (the processes/practices of representation), kitsch imitates *its effects*.

From this perspective, it is not too difficult to see why the constant tension between modernism and mass culture has moved in the direction of a postmodern dissolution of the distinction itself. The pace with which the market continues to commodify art forces the avant-garde to eventually run out of steam the more that novelty is tied to commercialism. Modern novelty has been transformed into the neoliberal mantra of "innovation."

The Frankfurt school and the culture industry

This concern with the market diffusion of art is also a recurrent theme in twentieth-century critical theory. In the mid-twentieth century, some of the most ardent critics of the market diffusion and commodification of modern art included theorists tied to the Institute for Social Research at the University of Frankfurt, otherwise known as the Frankfurt School. Two of the most prominent figures tied to the Frankfurt School were the social theorists Theodor Adorno and Max Horkheimer. In contrast to Habermas's lamenting of the incomplete project of modernity (he himself was a second generation Frankfurt School scholar), Adorno and Horkheimer argue in their book

Dialectic of Enlightenment (1944) that in fact the logical result of the modern project of Enlightenment has been its total and complete reversal, which they tie to the dual processes of instrumentalization (or, "instrumental reason") and commodification. Witnessing the mid-twentieth century rise of fascism and totalitarianism, both of which emerged out of instrumental interpretations of the Enlightenment project, Adorno and Horkheimer claim that the culmination of the Enlightenment project of rationalization is not freedom and emancipation; it is, rather, further (technocratic, bureaucratic) domination and control. In one of the key essays in this collection, "The Culture Industry: Enlightenment as Mass Deception,"[11] Adorno and Horkheimer argue, for instance, that the emergence of modern mass media such as cinema and radio have led to not a full-fledged, liberated democratic society, but instead, they claim, new media encourages the further integration of the population into the commodity culture of capitalism.

Adorno and Horkheimer coined the term "culture industry" in order to express the contradictions between modern industry (recall, for instance, the image of the Fordist assembly line), which commodifies and standardizes culture, and culture itself, which they see as that aspect of society which makes possible the subversion of domination ("make it new"). As supporters of the emancipatory value of modern art, they argue that the culture industry actually produces culture in the same way that it fashions the automobile and other mass goods, on an assembly line. Because it is mass produced, the culture industry robs culture of its authenticity. In its place, mass, popular, or "low" art confuses the mass production of art with democracy.

Certainly, contemporary new media have added new dimensions to Adorno and Horkheimer's culture industry thesis. The unidirectional communication of broadcast media has given way to the interactive spaces of social media such as Facebook and Twitter. The classical studio system has given way to new flexible models of production. Conglomeration in (now) the "cultural industries" includes online avenues of consumption such as YouTube and Netflix. Still, the processes

of commodification of culture, of which they were so critical, remain in full force with these apparently democratizing
aspects of contemporary new media.[12]

What is missing in commodified mass culture, according to
Adorno and Horkheimer, is a dimension of critical thought,
reflexivity, and awareness. Mass culture reproduces ideology as
a form of "false consciousness." For Adorno and Horkheimer,
the culture industry is opposed to modern art, which for them
is a critical practice that frees the individual from the con-
straints imposed by previous forms of domination, as well as
those developed in capitalist society. Modern art, as they see it,
is autonomous art. For them, modern art is a critical practice
capable of breaking free of the standardized, demoralizing culture of capitalism. Although they held an elitist conception of
modern art, they still saw it as much more critical and potentially revolutionary than mass culture, even though the latter's
appeal is more widespread, permeating the culture at large.
Adorno, Horkheimer, and the Frankfurt School more generally, are therefore exemplary of the kind of elitist criticism that
postmodernism tries to transgress. Adorno and Horkheimer
perceived a deep divide between modernism and mass culture,
where the latter is a mechanism for the diffusion of resistance,
emancipation, and critical thinking. However, their view of
modernism differs from the depoliticized version of it found
in earlier thinking about the avant-garde. Instead of "art for
art's sake," they see a revolutionary potential in modern art.
Postmodern critical theory similarly draws out the political in
culture; although now by dissolving the distinction between
high art and popular culture.

The movement from the kind of critical theory produced by
the Frankfurt School to postmodern theory involves a movement through film criticism and film theory. Film is in fact contradictory in the same way that the retroactive determination
of modern art by commodified mass culture is contradictory.
Film is very much a product of commodified mass culture and
emerged as one of the very first examples of the culture industry, especially due to the rise of the Hollywood studio system

in the first half of the twentieth century. But film has also been the subject of much of the modern art criticism that emerged in the postwar period, and it is in fact in the film and cultural theory of the later postwar period that some of the central questions and methods of postmodern theory were to develop.

Modernism, mass culture, and the cinema

The arrival of cinema is tied to the emergence of *both* modernism and mass culture in the late nineteenth and early twentieth centuries. As a new medium of representation, its form did not fully congeal until the second decade of the twentieth century. Initially, it was the spectacle of the medium itself that drew attention. But later, the medium developed into a narrative form of expression in itself. Early narrative cinema drew as well upon traditions in literature and theatre, staging at first famous works from these cultural fields. With the development of new film techniques, such as the continuity editing and establishing shots found in D. W. Griffith's *The Birth of a Nation* (1915) (a film that famously depicts the controversial glorification of the rise of the Ku Klux Klan), the Soviet montage techniques of Lev Kuleshov, and Sergei Eisenstein's theory of dialectical montage, found notably in *Battleship Potempkin* (1925) and *October: Ten Days That Shook the World* (1928), the cinema seemed to have found its own unique practices of representation.

Although film is a product of mass culture, the history of cinema shows us that it too has undergone historical shifts from an early realism, found in the examples cited above, toward its own modernism. The modern period of the silent era found expression in various international styles and auteurs, from the Soviet cinema of Eisenstein, to the German Expressionism of Robert Weine's *The Cabinet of Dr. Caligari* (1919), F. W. Murneau's *Nosferatu* (1922), and Fritz Lang's

Metropolis (1926). Modern movements also found expression in the surrealist films of Luis Buñuel and Salvador Dali, such as *Un Chien andelou* (1928) and *L'Age d'or* (1930), not to mention Maya Deren's *Meshes of the Afternoon* (1943). Dziga Vertov's experimental *The Man with a Movie Camera* (1929), a cinematic version of Russian constructivism, itself influenced by modern movements in design such as the Bauhaus and De Stijl, came out just prior to Stalin's demand to make Socialist Realism the official art of the Soviet Union.

We should also not discount the work of significant mass culture filmmakers such as Charlie Chaplin, Buster Keaton, and Cecile B. Demille, and their influence on modern film during the silent period. Charlie Chaplin's *Modern Times* (1936) and *The Great Dictator* (1940), for instance, are themselves marked by critical commentary on, not only the politics of the time, but also the changing culture brought on by modernization. *Modern Times* intriguingly and creatively deals with changing technologies in cinema, matched by its depiction of productive technologies in the factory. The film is considered silent since there is no spoken dialogue between the characters, though sound does play an important role in the film. Sounds and words emanate, not from characters, but from machines in the film. We do, in fact, hear spoken dialogue, though it is always mediated by a machine, whether a phonograph or a video monitor placed on the shop floor to properly monitor the workers in the factory. The commentary on modernization is evident, but it is Chaplin's formal use of sound that provides a further critique of the dehumanizing aspects of modern technology.

Other technological developments in postwar cinema had an impact on the character of modern film. With the advent of television and its growing popularity in the 1950s, film studios returned to a "cinema of attractions" model in a bid to revive interest in the medium. Color and widescreen were two such technological advantages that film had over television at the time. Along with these developments, a proliferation of genre films emerged in the 1950s. Though genre had been a part of prewar cinema, the postwar genre films developed as part of the mass culture and expansion of the postwar period, motivated by bigger budgets and the new spectacular technologies. Musicals, comedies, Westerns, gangster movies, and sci-fi films, all experienced revival in the cinema of this period, with added production values brought about by technological boom in sound, widescreen, and color techniques.

American Westerns grew in popularity, though in some cases they owed much to the Samurai films of Akira Kurosawa; for instance, John Sturge's *The Magnificent Seven* (1960) is a remake of Kurosawa's *The Seven Samurai* (1954), and the Italian "spaghetti Western," *A Fistful of Dollars* (1964), directed by Sergio Leone, is an almost shot-for-shot remake of Kurosawa's *Yojimbo* (1961). Though, it is John Ford's *The Searchers* (1956) that is perhaps the most paradigmatic example of the Western genre, starring John Wayne as the existential hero Ethan Edwards, a personality type typical as well of film noir style.

Film noir is less an actual genre than a category designated after the fact, in this case by a group of French film critics following the war. During the war, American films were banned in France, which was under German occupation. Following the war, when American films were again finally allowed to be screened in France, they came with "an emotional impact" unseen in previous cinema. These films, produced just prior to and during World War II, were so labeled because of their cynical and dark depiction of life, often with a downbeat and despairing atmosphere, characterized, at times, even by pessimism and nihilism. These were films that were also often highly scrutinized by the Hays Office, the informal self-regulatory censoring board that oversaw and managed the morality of depiction in American cinema. Wilder's *Double Indemnity* (1944), for instance, about an insurance salesman seduced by one of his clients, Phyllis Dietrichson—here, the typical figure of the "femme fatale"—who encourages him to murder her husband.

Science fiction was just as much a part of the postwar cinema as the gangster film and the Western, though sci-fi was often generally much more latently political than some of these other genres centering around the existential, nihilistic, and cynical hero. Science fiction has been a part of cinema even going back to *La Voyage dans la lune* and *Metropolis*. But the context of the Cold War in the 1950s is useful for thinking about the sci-fi depiction of the arrival of aliens and monsters on Earth, in films like *The Day the Earth Stood Still* (1951) and *Invasion of the Body Snatchers* (1956). The difference between prewar and postwar Sci-Fi can, again, be thought at the level of depiction, with the earlier films focusing more on the technological and scientific marvels of modernization, the rise of the modern city, and so forth, whereas postwar sci-fi dealt more with the political and human equation, sensibilities that were also impacted by the Cold War threat of nuclear catastrophe.

Cinema of this period was impacted also by the breakup of the big studios following the Hollywood antitrust case of 1948 that broke up the vertically integrated oligopolies of Paramount, and subsequently other major studios, and the ties that they had with theatre chains. As a result, the 1950s and 1960s saw a rise in independent film production. Also, due to an influx of foreign films that couldn't be as directly influenced by the Hays Office, the Production Code was ultimately scrapped, allowing for a change in the character of the stories depicted in American cinema. The result was a more overt depiction of sex and violence in cinema. A boom in avant-garde feature-length filmmaking in Europe, such as the French New Wave and Italian Neo-Realism, also signal the moment of high modernism in cinema, as does the recognition of film direction as a form of authorship, a point made clear in the "auteur theory" of the postwar French film critics.

I mention this context for a couple of reasons. The first is that it is necessary to see that, even though modern critics like Adorno and Horkheimer deem mass culture to be lacking in originality and authenticity, we do in fact see, within mass culture, an aesthetic shift from modernism to postmodernism. Early European cinema, the post–Hays Code Hollywood cinema, and the new postwar international cinemas, were very much a counterpart to modern movements in the other visual arts. The second is that, as we will see, one thing that distinguishes postmodern cinema is its reflexive use of genre and stereotypes of past genres. In the case of *Blade Runner*, for example, we see a combination of noir and sci-fi. Furthermore, it is the combination of newly emerging film and cultural theory in the postwar period with the arrival of film studies as a separate discipline in American and European universities in the late 60s and early 70s, which helped to institutionalize and legitimize film and film criticism in a way that makes possible postmodern theory and postmodern cinema. But just prior to its emergence, film and culture were politicized in a new way. Because the criticism of film has relied on methods from various disciplines, including studies of literature, sociology, political science, philosophy, and history, film is uniquely poised to be the basis for interdisciplinary, postmodern analysis of culture.

May '68 and after

As with the humanities and the arts in general, the study and criticism of film in the 1970s drew from the experiences of the decline of the postwar boom and the collapse of the social welfare state, but was significantly impacted by the events of May 1968 in Paris, and the squashing of the student and worker uprising. The mass student and worker protests in May '68 were prompted by the failed attempt by the French Communist and Socialist parties to remove the government of Charles de Gaulle. A few months earlier, Left groups in Paris occupied an administration building at the University of Paris at Nanterre to discuss problems of class discrimination in France, and were ultimately forced out by the police. After months of conflict between students and the administration, the university was shut down in May. Students groups came together in protest and were later joined by workers who occupied factories. Ultimately, the events of May '68 did not lead to any big revolutionary moment, and its failure was seen by many as a final blow to the utopian ideals of the old modern Left. But the events were successful to the extent that they encouraged cultural thinkers to repurpose the role of cultural theory and criticism. It is also in this moment that we begin to find some of the emergent elements of postmodern theory.

The failure of May '68 has been seen by some as marking the failure of the old Left in Europe, and is partially responsible for the kind of cynical resignation that has been part of the postmodern Left, which now shies away from big emancipatory projects, preferring smaller, more local sites of struggle. But May '68 has also prompted new approaches to cultural criticism. In their famous editorial in *Cahiers du cinema*, "Cinema/Ideology/Criticism," French film critics Jean-Louis Comolli and Jean Narboni make ideology critique of film the central objective of the kind of criticism that the journal was to publish in the period following May '68.[13] Ideological criticism now became a prominent force in the critique of culture, and we begin to see a return to a more interdisciplinary and holistic criticism of culture. However, with postmodernism, the underlying Marxist motivation behind the brand of ideological criticism found in Comolli and Narboni would fade, ideology critique—and later, "discourse analysis"—has remained as a central part of postmodern theory.

Structuralism and post-structuralism[14]

Other postwar theories and approaches, such as structuralism, so-called post-structuralism, and semiotics, were soon incorporated into the ideological criticism of film and culture. These were theories that diverged from the kind of formalism used to justify modern art. Instead of finding value in the formal aspects of art and culture, these methods sought to investigate the plurality of meanings in the text, or, in the work of some theorists these were methods used to *deconstruct* the meaning of the text.

Structuralism is a method used to analyze the underlying rules that organize social systems. In cultural analysis, it draws upon the work of the nineteenth-century Swiss linguist Ferdinand de Saussure, and the method that he developed, called "semiotics," or the science of signs, as well as the work of the mid-twentieth-century French structural anthropologist Claude Lévi-Strauss, who applied Saussure's methods to the study of culture. Saussure demonstrated that language could be understood at both a *synchronic* level—the level of language at a particular fixed moment in history—and a *diachronic* level—the changes that take place in language over time. Saussure was mainly interested in the synchronic level of language since it is only when language is fixed at a given moment that it can be understood as a *closed* structure, whereas diachronic language is constantly changing, and is therefore more difficult to study. Consider the English language, for instance. English is both open ended and dynamic: it is open ended because new words are constantly introduced (think about all of the new "e-" words and "i-" words that have entered into our everyday language in the digital age—e-mail, iPhone, etc.), and old words are constantly dropped; and it is dynamic because the meanings of words can change over time, based on new uses (think of how the hippie culture of the 1960s changed the meaning of the word "cool"). A synchronic analysis of language, however, leaves little room for thinking about the role of the subject in her *use* of language.

Post-structuralism, then, is a reaction against the synchronic and *a*subjective aspects of structuralism. For post-structuralism, history and subjectivity *are* in fact necessary elements of analysis. Furthermore, post-structuralism has an interest in seeing how power plays a role in fixing language and meaning *within* a given and particular historical moment. Post-structuralism also rejects the way that structuralism understood the organization of social structures through *binary oppositions*. Jacques

Derrida, a leading figure in post-structuralism, argued that in every binary opposition (such as male/female), one of the terms in the binary is given more significance, so that the one term—the transcendental signified—defines the opposition itself. For this reason, post-structuralists took the semiotic distinction between the *signifier*—the word- or sound-image that names an object (i.e., "tree")—and the *signified*—the object or thing itself (i.e., an actual tree)—and inverted their significance, giving priority to the signifier, preferring to think of meaning as the result of a constant *play* of signifiers. Part of the practice of thinking of history from a post-structuralist perspective is thus considering the role of the signifier and of power in fixing meaning in history.

Screen theory and Cultural Studies

Along with structuralism and semiotics, Lacanian psychoanalysis became a staple method of film analysis in the pages of the British film journal, *Screen*, in the 1970s, which combined Marxist analyses of ideology with psychoanalytic and structuralist conceptions of the subject in order to develop a notion of the cinematic spectator.[15] This was partially inspired by the events of May '68, but also by the work of the French philosopher Louis Althusser, whose concept of ideological state apparatuses (ISAs), which made use of psychoanalysis for his theory of ideology, encouraged cultural thinkers to view cinema as one such ISA, responsible for transforming spectators into subjects of ideology. With its concern for the spectator, film and cultural theory started giving some attention back to audiences, whereas modern criticism focused primarily on the artist.

The British film theorist Laura Mulvey published an article in 1975, "Visual Pleasure in Narrative Cinema," which is one of the first major attempts to use psychoanalysis to develop a critique, not of the class basis of cinematic subjecthood, but of the gendered aspect of depiction and interpellation.[16]

According to her, mainstream Hollywood cinema produces a "male gaze," where spectators come to view the film from the perspective of the male protagonist. Mulvey's theory of spectatorship, along with other similar arguments in *Screen*, came to be called "screen theory," and was later criticized heavily for viewing spectators as merely passive vessels for the absorption of ideology. This was a perspective that was criticized by a group of British cultural thinkers working at the Centre for Contemporary Cultural Studies at the University of Birmingham, contemporaries with the screen theorists.

Rather than seeing spectatorship as a process of passive indoctrination, Cultural Studies focuses attention on the actual conditions of viewing, including the social, political, and cultural contexts of viewers. Cultural Studies, for instance, places emphasis on the role that race, class, and gender play on the reception, or "decoding," of a cultural text. Just as screen theory was influenced by the political context of May '68 and the aspiration to provide an ideological critique of cultural objects, Cultural Studies was likewise influenced by the politics of the 1960s and the rise of the new social movements and the New Left. By adding the dimension of race and gender to that of class, and the role that each played in the reception of the text, Cultural Studies gave priority to the cultural conditions in which reception took place, and in which pleasure was received by the audience. In this way, Cultural Studies' emphasis on pluralism translated into the postmodern concern for plural and parallel interpretations of the text. Cultural Studies and the new social movements, particularly postcolonialism, antiracism, and feminism, are also partially responsible for the rise of the "culture wars" in European and American universities, which are said to have displaced the earlier attention to traditional and high culture. Therefore, the 60s and 70s, the events of May '68, the rise of the new social movements, the New Left in Europe, and finally the institutional challenges to traditional culture—the entry of feminism, post-colonialism, antiracism, and film studies itself—make it possible now to see where and how postmodernism emerged in the postwar period. Nevertheless, as I have been arguing from the beginning, the feature that finally distinguishes postmodernism from modernism is its approach to history.

The end of history

Postmodernism is first and foremost interested in history. But it is the very conceptualization of the term "history" that becomes *a*—if not *the*—central problematic for postmodern theorists, critics, and scholars. When we refer to "history" are we talking about all of history? Are we speaking about some objective/neutral presentation of events that happened in the past? What is the relationship between the past, the present, and the future? Are we capable of even understanding something about the direction of human history simply by researching and studying the past, examining events in the present, and projecting future possibilities? What are the limitations placed on such endeavors? When we speak about "history" are we talking about a single unified (global) history, or are we referring to a partial history viewed from the perspective of the West? Whose history? Are we discussing "history" or (capital "H") "History"? The latter implying some kind of authoritative stance about history.

Evoking questions about authority, postmodern thinkers question the subjective stance of dominant historical narratives. History, they say, never comes from some purely neutral/objective perspective. History is always written by the oppressor (or so the saying goes). What about history or histories (plural) from below? Questions about authority, and the authoritative writing of history invokes, as well, questions about subjectivity, since it might be acknowledged that history is always written from a perspective that is partial rather than total—total histories, where the author seems to be speaking for the other, always appearing oppressive and leaving out the perspective of the vanquished. Stemming from a partial subjective position, it must also be noted that history is often, as well, read against some kind of ideology or theoretical stance. Regardless of whether it is a religious, secular, emancipatory, or progressive ideology, postmodernism tries to make apparent the fact that history, coming from a subjective stance that is partial, brought up to a position of authority, is always still a *representation* of the past, present, and potential future that is portrayed and structured by an ideological or theoretical paradigm. Since all history is partial, since it is always ideological, can we even locate some underlying historical truth or essence? The postmodern answer is an unequivocal "no!" Bearing all of this in mind, we might say that the statement that best captures this postmodern stance on history is the one made famous by the American neoconservative scholar Francis Fukuyama, that we have reached the "end of history."[17]

Though his statement comes a couple of decades later than when I wish to date the emergence of postmodernism as a school of thought, as an ideology, and as a name for an aspect of contemporary culture, the thesis about the "end of history" is a good place to start our discussion of postmodernism. Fukuyama made this statement in the dying days of the Cold War. By claiming that we have reached the end of history, Fukuyama is not by any means claiming that events will not continue to accumulate; nor does it imply that important historical moments will cease to occur. Rather, his point is that we have reached the end of history in the sense of searching for the best models—political and economic—for organizing society. With the end of the Cold War and the collapse of the Soviet Union in the late 1980s and early 1990s, it looked as though the world had finally settled on liberal democracy in politics and a market economy. All that remained were a few "clashes of civilization," referring to conflicts between Western/Northern powers and states/terrorist groups in the Middle East. But, as this logic went, all that these outsiders have to do is to integrate themselves into the global liberal democratic and market orders, and we will finally arrive at "utopia."

Fukuyama's claim about the end of history is based on a particular reading of the work of the German philosopher

G. W. F. Hegel, for whom history tends toward some rational progressive direction, which in his *Logic* he refers to as "absolute knowing." History, in this sense, is a history of ideas—of ideas about progress and knowledge, where it can, in the last instance, become possible to obtain or gain some clear sense of absolute/total understanding. Hegel's dialectical method and view of history influenced the view of history developed by Karl Marx as well. We might say that for Marx—or at least, in one interpretation of Marx and Marxism—the end of history would come with the arrival of Communism. Fukuyama's end of history argument is similar to that of Marx, except that for him, the demise of the Soviet Union and the victory of capitalism in those years meant that Marx was wrong, that capitalism itself *is* the end of history. The apparent victory of liberal democracy and of capitalism signaled, then, in a way, the final fulfillment of a human project of emancipation and progress that began with the European Enlightenment. This, we might say, is where the postmodernists depart quite substantially from Fukuyama.

Although it is possible to characterize the postmodern sensibility toward History with reference to Fukuyama's "end of history" thesis, postmodernism takes this argument a step further. Postmodernism shares with Fukuyama a critique of the Marxist conception of History, though the postmodernists are equally critical of liberal conceptions of History, or any understanding of History that is teleological, leading toward some ultimate sense of completion, or even drawing out some underlying sense of *origin* or *essence*. Critical postmodernists, then, view the "end of history" more literally, not as the end of the historical progress toward some goal. Postmodernism, as we have seen, can be characterized as an "incredulity toward metanarratives," or "grand narratives." The problem that postmodernists have with grand narratives are, as I have already alluded to above, their tendency toward being authoritative, creating an appearance of objectivity and neutrality, linking to some essence or origin that will find redemption in the future, when in fact they are quite subjective and ideological, representing some partial perspective of truth. Both the liberal conception of history and the Marxist conception fall into this problematic. But equally, for postmodernists, do theories about morality, identity, and subjectivity, such as the Judeo-Christian tradition, Freudian psychoanalysis, and structural linguistics. Postmodernists therefore, alongside a pluralistic view of history, speak also about "knowledges" and epistemologies, subject positions, and identities in the plural, without any inclination toward fixation or centralization.

Though it can first be conceptualized through its perspective on history, postmodernism is also a term that can be used to describe a particular cultural sensibility and an aesthetic. Jameson has pointed out that the discussion surrounding the end of history has largely replaced discussions about another "end": the discussion about the "end of art."[18] One way to interpret the latter, according to him, is to look at the final fate of those various art movements from the mid-nineteenth to the mid-twentieth century grouped together under the term "modern." Modern art, according to Jameson, "ends" precisely at the moment when postmodernism begins to emerge. But in what sense?

As we have seen, modern art is often described as those aesthetic practices that are bound by an ethic of novelty. Modern art was constantly obsessed with transcending older boundaries and challenging authority. But what happens when modern art, driven by its ethic of transcendence and challenge to authority, as well as its vocation to not be commodity and to go beyond those market efforts to commodify art, turns itself into kitsch and popular commercial art—what happens when this art becomes *the* official art, canonized in the museums, the universities, and the dominant state institutions? The fact that modern art met this fate is, according to Jameson, one way to interpret the end of *modern* art.

The "end of art" thesis was also, a century and a half prior to the end of *modern* art, a topic of debate for Hegel in his lectures on aesthetics. According to Jameson, the end of art, for Hegel, meant the rising authority of philosophy. Art "ends," and what takes its place in the pursuit of the absolute is pre-cisely philosophical thought and discourse. The art specific to Hegel's argument was romanticism, itself emerging out of the failure of Christianity to reach the absolute. Jameson's thesis is that there was an "event" that Hegel wanted to refer to as the end of art that did emerge after the failure of romantic art to reach the absolute, but that this event did not signal the rise of philosophy; instead it led to the rise of modern-ism and modern art, which held onto an ethic that was quite different from that of romanticism and romantic formalism. But it is worth conceptualizing the difference between roman-ticism and modernism in terms drawn out by Immanuel Kant. That is, the difference between *the beautiful* and *the sublime*. The former having to do much more with the immediate aes-thetic pleasure derived from the form and direct content of the art object, whereas the sublime is something that goes deeper and even beyond the immediate encounter with the object. The sublime is beyond words, beyond discourse. It addresses the uncanny and perhaps irrational aspects of the natural world that are beyond the cognitive understanding of the human subject. Romanticism is an art of the beautiful; modernism is an art of the sublime. The end of art that Hegel foresaw was therefore, according to Jameson, the end of the beautiful in art. The "end," though, of modern art, brings with it another "end." What gets lost with the end of modern art, according to Jameson, is *the vocation of art to reach the absolute.*

Just as Hegel believed philosophy to be the natural inheritor of art's ending, so too Jameson believes that what has come to be called *Theory*—that is, structuralism, structural Marxism, and so on,—has in fact been taken up in the wake of modern art's diffusion into the official cannon. What happens when the sublime is desublimated by itself becoming the norm or the authoritative? Theory, says Jameson, emerged as a product of the philosophical engagement with modern art, but proceeded from it and gained authenticity in the wake of the demise of modernism. However, its arrival comes in parallel with the emergence of the postmodern.

The postmodern, from this discussion, can be understood as that brand of art and culture that emerges when modern art itself becomes the authoritative model of all art, and therefore something to resist. Paradoxically, modern art, driven by its challenges to authority, *becomes authority*, and as a reaction formation we end up with what has thereafter been called "postmodern." Postmodernism, in other words, is what happens when subversion (of authority) becomes the norm. Modern art, in this sense, does not end by becoming nothing, but by becoming "everything." So, in what sense is postmodernism a practice of resistance if practices of resistance are now part of the official ideology?

Michel Foucault's critique of "ideology" and "repression"

To simplify, there are four main areas of criticism, tied to modernism, at which postmodern takes aim: ideology, authority, subjectivity, and history. They can be discerned in the work of the French social theorist Michel Foucault and his critiques of Marxism and psychoanalysis, particularly the concepts of ideology and repression. From this critique, other postmodern targets of modernism can be discerned. For Foucault, the Marxist concept of *ideology* is problematic for the following reasons: (1) Ideology is too often opposed to "truth"; (2) Ideology is tied to the concept of the subject; and, (3) Ideology is said to be determined by some underlying economic base.[19] The Marxist and psychoanalytic conceptions of *repression* are, for Foucault, equally problematic. According to him, if power is defined in terms of repression, in terms of a power that says "no," then we end up ignoring the *productive* aspects of power.

Foucault's critique of ideology immediately identifies three other elements of the postmodern critique of modernism. The first is the fact that ideology is opposed to some conception of "truth." In other words, according to him, there is for those who draw on the concept of ideology in their critique of power, oppression, and exploitation, an underlying reality that counts as truth—or a "true consciousness," an "essence" beneath the appearance—and then there is ideology that counts as a kind of "false consciousness." Foucault's critique of ideology as "false consciousness" is dependent, as well, upon his methodological commitment to the study of "truth effects" in different *discourses*. According to Foucault, truth and truths are the result of different historical forms of *knowledge* (discourses), produced by figures of *authority*, or experts, within a given field of knowledge (recall Habermas's schema above that divides different fields of inquiry into degrees of expertise). Religion, for instance, produces discourses about morality, grounded in the authoritative voice of the clergy; the psychiatric clinic produces discourses about normal and abnormal behavior through the authoritative voice of the psychiatrist; and so forth. Rather than some underlying truth, in other words, we have various different *truths* that are discursively produced, reflective of some structuring authoritative voice, or power, providing and authorizing the legitimacy of that truth. It is, however, the framework of knowledge, according to Foucault, that determines the truth, or (to use a term coined by Stephen Colbert) the "truthiness," of a given object. Rather than some neutral objective truth found by the experts in the discipline, Foucault is keen to point toward a subjective dimension that informs the truth effect found in the discourse, and in this way creates an axis of power–knowledge. From this we get our second element of the postmodern reaction to modernism: *authority*.

Though he is critical of this word, Foucault might say that every ideology is dependent upon, or reflective of, not some underlying truth, but some overarching authority. Ideology is tied to authority in Foucault's criticism of power as repression, as a power that says "no!" Power, for Foucault, is not merely a repressive force; power is also a productive force, particularly in the way that power–knowledge produces subject positions, forms of desire and resistance, through discursive practices and constructions. Power is not simply a matter of the macro-authority of the state; it is also to be located in the micro-institutions, or "disciplines" such as the prison, the clinic, and the church. Taking account of what we have said so far, we see that for Foucault, "discourse" replaces ideology and "discipline" replaces authority.

The second point in Foucault's critique of ideology, and the third target of the postmodern critique of modernism, is *subjectivity*. There is, here, an implicit reference to Althusser who claimed that ideology *interpellates* individuals as subjects. For Althusser, subjectivity is an imaginary construction. People are transformed into subjects of ideology when they identify with and conform to the very terms produced to create compliance toward authority. The modern subject is imagined as an autonomous individual with rights sanctioned by the law. But, as both Foucault and Althusser might argue, the law is a discursive formation that produces the category of the subject, somewhat tautologically, as its own self-justification. Subject, for Althusser, is a category that emerges from bourgeois ideology, and is nothing but an imaginary representation of the individual. It is in this way tied to ideology. Foucault, then, likewise sees the subject as a product of discourse.

The last point in Foucault's critique of ideology is *infrastructure*. With this term, Foucault is referring to the Marxist conception of the *base and superstructure*. An orthodox Marxist perspective argues that we can understand a society in the abstract by referring to different levels: the base, and the superstructure. Both the base and the superstructure refer to ways of understanding the relationships between people in society, but the same population is understood differently depending upon whether we are referring to the base or the superstructure. The "base" refers to a society's *mode of production*. From the Marxist perspective, in order for any society to exist and to continue to exist, it must constantly reproduce itself materially. The mode of production of a society refers to both the materials necessary for the production and reproduction of a society, or means of production, and the relations of production, that is, the social relationships between people that organize the different jobs, or roles that people play in the production/reproduction of society. The relations of production are often, historically, divided between mental and manual labor—between those who do the planning, and those who execute those plans. Marx argued that all of history is the history of class struggles. Relations of production point toward *political* class struggles, as the division of labor is usually between those who rule a society and those who are ruled; between those who oppress/exploit others, and those who are oppressed/exploited. In the context of the relations of production, it is usually the ruling class that owns or controls the means of production.

The superstructure refers to the same people that make up the population, but looks at the relationships between people in a different way. The superstructure is made up of all of the various institutions that form a society, such as the state, family, religion, education, culture, and the media (to name only a few). The Marxist perspective argues that the superstructure is reflective of the relations of production in the base, and for some this means that the base *determines* the superstructure. For instance, the state and legal apparatus in a capitalist society creates and backs up the laws that make possible the continued domination of the capitalist class over the exploited working class. This is contained in laws about private property, for instance. The superstructure, then, is the sphere of culture and ideology that supports the interests of the ruling class in the base. This is why, as Foucault puts it, "ideology" is in a *secondary position* to the infrastructure, or the base. Though, if the superstructure were fully determined by the base, there would be little room for resistance, and hence class struggle would not exist. Althusser argued, then, that there was a "relative autonomy" between the base and the superstructure. Although the superstructure is reflective of the base, room still exists to resist the relations of domination in the mode of production, and in other social, political, and cultural spheres of society.

Foucault's critique of the tie between ideology and the infrastructure/base leads us toward the fourth, and as I've been arguing, most significant target of modernism: History. Drawing on the work of the philosopher Friedrich Nietzsche, Foucault challenged the Marxist view of history. The Marxist conception of history can be understood in two ways: (1) As the history of class struggles; (2) As the historical movement from one underlying mode of production to the next. The movement from one mode of production to the next arises out of the inherent contradictions of the previous mode of production, accompanied by a revolutionary rupture that transforms the underlying relations of production. Foucault challenges this notion of history, preferring Nietzsche's genealogical method, which opposes the search for origins and truth—thus we are back to the first point about ideology. For Foucault, historical materialism—the Marxist approach—sees historical analysis as the search for truths and origins in society's base/infrastructure. His genealogical approach is thus averse to this for the same reason that he is opposed to the theory of ideology: origins are themselves postulated by authoritative positions within a discursive formation. Instead of an ideology arising out of the relationship between the historical transformations of the base, we have a series of free-floating discourses, tied together by forms of power–knowledge.

History, authority, subjectivity, and ideology—these are the four primary elements of modernism that postmodernism seeks to challenge, and from these points of negation, we can now discern the central targets of postmodern theory. From the relationship between authority and History, we find the postmodern interest in critiquing "master narratives," which can be understood as discourses of history expressive of a particular assemblage of power–knowledge. Furthermore, postmodernism comes to understand modern master narratives of history as postulated by a particular subjective position—one modelled on the Cartesian category of the subject (the famous "I think, therefore I am"), or the centered, liberal subject of the Enlightenment, classed by the bourgeoisie, and evidently masculine and European. Although Marxism and psycho-analysis share with postmodernism a critique of the modern bourgeois subject, both have become primary targets of post-modern theory because they are still categorized as modern master narratives.

Against master narratives

Historical materialism and psychoanalysis have become two of the main targets of postmodern criticism. Drawing on Nietzsche, Foucault sought to displace the Marxian concep-tion of history as both the history of class struggles and the his-torical transition from one mode of production to the next.[20] He was also concerned with critiquing modern theories, which located power in "megastructures" such as the state, or a rul-ing class. Not only was he critical of the Marxist conception of history and power, he saw as equally problematic the liberal Enlightenment conception of history as rational and progres-sive, or, in other words, as teleological. In Nietzsche's geneal-ogy Foucault saw a method that attempted to rethink the social from a micro perspective, one that allows for closer examina-tion of discursive discontinuity, rather than the implied conti-nuity and identity of grand narrative. In his essay "Nietzsche, Genealogy, History," Foucault sets out a practice for thinking history that goes against the endeavor to locate origins and con-tinuous, linear historical progression. Instead of relying on a base/superstructure model of historical investigation, in which, from this perspective, history originates in the political class struggle, Foucault's genealogical method understands history as the development of discursive "truths," formed often at the intersection of a plurality of overlapping influences and traces. Genealogy opposes terms associated with grand narrative, like civilization and epoch, historical period, as well as concep-tions of a centered subject of history. Genealogical history is opposed to the so-called total histories, attributed to figures like Hegel and Marx. While the dislodging of metanarrative is, for both Lyotard (as we saw in the Introduction) and Foucault, tied to the historical narratives of liberalism and Marxism, it is toward Freud and psychoanalysis that Gilles Deleuze and Felix Guattari turn in the anti-interpretivism of their book *Anti-Oedipus* (1972).

Deleuze and Guattari remain critical of metanarrative in much the same way as Lyotard and Foucault; and, although they find problematic the dialectical method of historical materialism, they still draw upon a Marxist critique of capitalism to produce what they see as one of the primary mechanisms of power in bourgeois society: Freudian psychoanalysis. For them, psychoanalysis is a process of trying to reconstitute, or "territorialize" (fix), desire by grounding it in the artificial form of the nuclear family: the "mommy-daddy-me" relationship, as they put it.[21] According to them, Freud makes family life and the Oedipus complex central to psychic development. However, drawing upon Jacques Lacan, who in his early work reinterpreted Freud using structural linguistics, Deleuze and Guattari point to the signifying processes of the psychoanalytic model of repression. Lacan reinterpreted the Oedipus complex as a linguistic, rather than a biological phenomenon. Instead of the biological father, Lacan emphasized the function of the "Name-of-the-Father" in the order of language—or the Symbolic order—marked by a master-signifier—a signifier without signified that *constitutes* the field of language and meaning itself. The master-signifier, in other words, artificially closes the loop of meaning, the unhinging of which would detotalize meaning.

Using categories developed both by Nietzsche and Marx—power and economics—Deleuze and Guattari outline three social formations: savagery, despotism, and capitalism, which shouldn't be understood as stages of history but as three different types of social organization. Deleuze and Guattari describe these three social formations by addressing the level of "coding" in each. Savagery, though heavily coded—which Deleuze and Guattari interpret as highly repressive—is still relatively egalitarian, since it seeks not to accumulate power, a fact that distinguishes it from despotism. The latter is based upon codes that establish hierarchy and class divisions. Here, the Name-of-the-Father enters to organize the Symbolic order, into the patriarchal domination of the nuclear family. Capitalism, in contrast, has no such central point of fixation, no transcendental signified. According to Deleuze and Guattari, economic exchange in the market undermines all fixed meanings and social codes. Capitalism, in this sense, provides a "decoding" and deterritorialization—or "lines of flight"—from despotic forms of repression. However, the potentially emancipatory effects of deterritorialization stemming from market exchange in a capitalist society are still accompanied, according to Deleuze and Guattari, by processes of territorialization stemming from positions of power. Psychoanalysis, for Deleuze and Guattari, is one such metanarrative of re-territorialization. What they call "schizoanalysis" is a critical practice that seeks to eliminate repressive practices of recoding, which help to reinforce the power of capitalists. One of the main thrusts of the postmodern theory of art and culture is thus the refusal to recode.

Schizoanalysis is an "anti-interpretivist" method that offers a postmodern critique of the modern practices of recoding, for instance, in the formation of the autonomous bourgeois individual subject. It opposes interpretation since the latter reinforces codes and master narratives, like Oedipus and historical materialism. Instead of interpretation, schizoanalysis aims to highlight strategies of ideological closure and the containment of desire, strategies that point toward sites of power. Deleuze and Guattari's anti-interpretivist method, and their championing of the schizo therefore provide Jameson with a model for further conceptualizing postmodernism, even historically. Drawing inspiration from them, Jameson uses the Lacanian model for psychosis/schizophrenia—as a "breakdown of the signifying chain"—to describe the postmodern incredulity toward grand narrative.

The breakdown of the signifying chain

For Lacan, the "signifying chain," or the Symbolic order, is the field of language and meaning. It represents, as well, the written and unwritten rules of a society, often reified or objectified into figures of authority, such as judges, police officers, experts, and so on. When these figures speak in their official roles, it is almost as if the Symbolic order (what Lacan also referred to as the "big Other") is speaking through them. However, postmodernism, as we saw earlier, marks a historical moment in which the authority of these figures starts to wane, at least as *sources* of ideological authority, particularly in the realm of art and culture. The "breakdown of the signifying" chain—or what Slavoj Žižek has alternatively referred to as the "demise of symbolic efficiency"[22]—therefore makes sense as an aesthetic representation of postmodernism, generally. In semiotic terms, what this means is that the master-signifier, the key signifier maintaining closure and certainty of the Symbolic, is troubled and loses its authority (i.e., the Name-of-the-Father), therefore opening up the entire field of signification and meaning; and this is precisely what postmodernism seeks to do. The authority of what? Well, as the name would seem to indicate, the authority that is undermined with the postmodern is that of modernism itself. Although modernism, too, was concerned with the dislodging of authority, we might say that postmodernism is what emerges when the challenge to authority *becomes* the norm. When the subversion of authority itself seemingly becomes the authoritative position. This puts postmodern criticism in a difficult position, and is one reason why it is often charged with being overly relativistic.

The result of this breakdown of the signifying chain, according to Jameson[23]—that is, of the loss of reference against which the culture can conceive itself—is the rise of a new kind of depthlessness and flatness. Unlike the modern depth models and thematics of alienation, anomie, solitude, social fragmentation, and isolation (tied to modernism as the so-called age of anxiety), postmodernism emphasizes "practices," discourses, and textual play or "intertextuality." Postmodernism, according to Jameson, replaces depth with surface or a multitude of surfaces, and this is so because—as suggested by the model of the breakdown of the signifying chain—postmodernism no longer has a referent (the master-signifier) against which to base itself. There is no underlying *essence*, and, in fact, any attempt to define essence is deemed a priori inadmissible since it would seem to suggest priority to some kind of authoritative voice.

Jameson identifies four depth models that have waned with the arrival of postmodernism:

1. The dialectic between essence and appearance
2. The psychoanalytic model of repression
3. The existential model of authenticity/inauthenticity, or of alienation/disalienation, and
4. The semiotic opposition between signifier and signified.

This last model—of the opposition between the signifier and signified—seems to overdetermine the rest, at least in terms of the semiotic language he uses to describe the postmodern. With the loss of reference to the master-signifier, there ceases to be any sense within postmodernism for identifying a deeper realm of authenticity, alienation, affect, or essence. In these terms, two points of reference appear prominent, the loss of which helps to characterize the aesthetic of the postmodern: the subject and History.

With postmodernism, the alienation of the subject seems to have been replaced by the *fragmentation* of the subject—that is, with the "death of the subject" it seems as if there is no longer any subject present (really) to experience feelings of alienation, anomie, solitude, and so on. There are two notions of the death of the subject at play here: the historicist one in which the loss referred to is that of the centered bourgeois subject of the nuclear, conjugal family—this is a loss pronounced even in modernity with Freud's discovery of the unconscious. The second—the post-structural model—is however, perhaps much more radical, suggesting that the subject never actually existed in the first place and is in reality a mere effect of discourse. The discursive conception of the subject, which in different ways draws upon the Althusserian conception of interpellation and the Foucauldian conception of discipline and power, has played a critical role in decisively undermining the authority of the modern artist/author, as well as any sense of authenticity/uniqueness in postmodernity.

With the death of the subject there is a parallel death of *unique style*. This is not so dissimilar to the argument proposed earlier that postmodernism arrives at the moment of total commodification, when negation is no longer possible because, on the one hand, there is no longer anything that is not commodity, and, on the other hand, because, at least at the level of style, everything that can be done has *already* been done. Whereas the ethic of modernism was to "make it new," postmodernism is what we get when there is nothing radically new to make; newness becomes redoubled, relying on the quotation, the sample (as in Hip Hop music), and the reference—but the type of reference is precisely what is at stake in the second referent point lost: the loss of History. The loss of reference to authority (i.e., the master-signifier, the Name-of-the-Father) and the loss of reference to History are productive of postmodern populism, and the stylistic conventions of pastiche and parody. Although postmodern populism was noticeable in various fields of art and culture, it was first found and most pronounced in architecture.

Postmodernism and populism

Postmodern architecture is both an attempt to distance itself from the Enlightenment tradition of "progress," *and* a reactionary impulse toward the preindustrial past. The term "postmodern" was used in architecture to describe new practices in contemporary buildings that, unlike the formalism, functionalism, and rationalism of the International Style (the epitome of modern architecture), returned to practices of ornamentation, beautification, and the reference to traditional styles, local histories, and the vernacular. Though it is sometimes difficult to see the strict differences between modernism and postmodernism, partly because the latter seeks to parody and therefore often appropriates from modern (as well as popular) aesthetics, the distinctions are most evident in architecture. It is in architecture, too, that we can locate the political consequences of modernism as symptomatic of capitalism's inherent drive toward growth and expansion. The modern ethic to "make it new" fits perfectly with relentless capitalist development. In order for capital to expand, it must constantly break down and overcome barriers to expansion, not unlike the modern quest to constantly negate the old. Postmodern architecture thus negates modernism by returning to classical and traditional styles and the construction and design of individual buildings, rather than the broader design and planning of total urban space.

The modern avant-garde, in a way, then shares with capitalism a Faustian developmental imperative that dialectically seeks to destroy the past in order to pave the way to the future. The avant-garde, in this sense, paralleled, and without knowing it, necessarily partook in the modernizing agenda of capitalism, which is itself invested in negating the old, and perpetually creating new needs and the products that can satisfy these (false) needs. Capitalism thrives, not only by obliterating and building on top of an older material environment, but also through the creation of new subjectivities, personalities, and identities, ones that break with traditional values, and lead toward new practices of consumption. While capitalism survives through exploitation, it is, as Marx and Engels note in *The Communist Manifesto*, highly contradictory and responsible for destroying older ideologies and antagonisms, and creating emancipatory possibilities for the exploited. While locating new modern identities in practices of consumption, postmodernism responds by appropriating and critiquing the products of a commodity culture. But the extent to which its own practices of appropriation avoid the risk of being incorporated into the consumer culture of late capitalism is a pressing concern.

Certainly, a defining feature of postmodernism has been its propensity toward closing the gap between high art or culture and "low," mass or popular culture. In a way, this has been made possible by new communication technologies like television (and, a bit later, the internet), whereby works of art have indeed been "democratized" and have been made available to the larger population. Postmodernism lacks an avant-garde or revolutionary impulse, and is often accused of surrendering to commodification and the market. However, the anti-avant-gardist stance of postmodern theorists, artists, and cultural producers is still highly conscientious, seeking instead to expand and explore different uses of new media.[24] Postmodern art tries to play with popular culture in a way that was previously absent. It therefore takes seriously the culture of the masses, while simultaneously trying to evoke practices of reflection. The work of the photographer Cindy Sherman is exemplary. Her series of film stills, for instance, *evoke* pop images by staging scenes that look like they might be taken from popular films in the 1940s or 1950s. If we consider the de-territorializing aspects of postmodernism, it is possible to understand how the market forces of late capitalism allow for this type of blending of high and low culture.

Another aspect of postmodernism that distinguishes it from modern art is its conception of "culture." Culture, as the Cultural Studies scholar Raymond Williams put it, "is ordinary."[25] Culture, in other words, is not only the high culture, or high art, of the museum or the gallery. Culture is also what describes our everyday way of life and the practices that make up daily living. This sense of culture is therefore much more inclusive than the modern notion of (capital 'C') Culture, and includes elements of mass and popular culture, which, within the context of a capitalist society, *is* a commodified, commercialized culture. If art is to have anything to do with this sense of culture, then it must reflect the actually lived commodified culture of late capitalism. Therefore, postmodernism does break down barriers between art and kitsch; it does break down the barriers between the avant-garde and advertising. Postmodernism, then, according to Jameson, can be characterized as a form of "aesthetic populism."[26]

Aesthetic populism is an expression that allows us, on the one hand, to consider the collapse between high art and popular culture, and, on the other hand, it provides a basis for dissolving what Jameson calls "critical distance." That is to say, with postmodernism, the relative autonomy that separated the cultural sphere from the economic seems to have disappeared. According to Jameson, this has come as a result of the changes brought forth by late capitalism. His Marxist view of postmodernism therefore still holds to a historical materialist conception of periodization, and for him, it is the result of the structuring influence of changes made to the capitalist mode of production. In this case, the culture of late capitalism has allowed for the total commodification of space, therefore making it near impossible to locate any culture, high or popular, that is not touched by the growing influence of multinational capitalism. Culture and commodity are now inseparable. However, what this means for a postmodern critique of cinema is that we are not bound only to the culture of the avant-garde. Instead, postmodernism makes popular culture its object of analysis, while, at the same time, popular culture has incorporated forms, styles, techniques, and themes from an older modernism. As we will see, this conception of postmodernism helps us to understand how to conceive *Blade Runner* as a quintessential example of postmodern cinema.

Pastiche and parody

Postmodernism's reference to history and its loss is also quite specific. With postmodernism, we are not talking about the loss of any historical reference, as such—and on this point, the differences between Jameson and the Canadian literary scholar Linda Hutcheon are significant—but with the loss of (capital "H") History, or the so-called grand narratives/metanarratives of modernism, such as historical materialism, or bourgeois liberalism. Alongside Foucault's genealogical method, postmodernism espouses a conception of history that relies more on the discursive model of multiple sources rather than a unique origin. Stylistically, according to Jameson, this conception of the loss of historical reference helps us to understand the postmodern replacement of parody with pastiche. While with parody the reference is obvious and recognizable, locatable in its historical original, pastiche is a mode of referencing the past—past styles—but in a way that eviscerates the original.

Pastiche is a form of quotation *without* reference. Since the referent is lost—particularly a historical and/or political one—the quotations found in representations as pastiche seem familiar, but in an amnesiac way. Again, Cindy Sherman's film stills are exemplary. Her stills seem to be taken from specific 1950s/1960s black-and-white films—they look familiar—but they are in fact recreations of films that never existed in the first place. Their reference is nonexistent. They play with style—that is, there is a resemblance to modern styles and genres, but the source code gets lost somehow. This is because, as Jameson puts it, modernist *styles* have become postmodern *codes*. The modernist style has become, in other words, a code for encoding the postmodern image.

In part, the loss of reference is due to the postmodern collapses of history and ideology. This is so since power in postmodern society seems to operate in disguise. In place of the older, liberal, industrial bourgeoisie, the era of late capitalism is dominated by new faceless masters, so to speak. Again, there is a loss of reference to authority, in part sparked by the injunction in consumer society for obligated enjoyment. Without a truly visible ruling class, the practice of parody becomes less and less viable. In its place is pastiche, which is like parody in its manner of imitation, but loses much of the potency of the latter since its referent is neutralized.

Hutcheon argues, in contrast, that postmodern parody *does* in fact acknowledge the historical past, and uses irony as a way of practicing the political in postmodernism.[27] She claims, instead, that there is a double process in postmodern parody, of installing and of ironizing. Installing is a way of showing that representations in the present originate in the past, while irony is used to identify the ideological underpinnings of past representations. However, keeping with the postmodern theme of challenging origins and underlying essences, postmodern parody calls into question conceptions of originality and value. Instead, postmodernism uses irony to acknowledge the fact that we are distanced from past ideologies. Postmodern parody is thus *doubly-coded*: politically, it both legitimizes *and* subverts what it parodies. It is a kind of "authorized transgression." It can be, therefore, self-reflexive, but at the same time is bound by historical and aesthetic conventions.

Representation and reflexivity

Unlike modern art and culture, which sought to distance itself from the political and the ideological, creating an autonomous sphere, postmodernism is more self-reflexive of its own political and ideological contexts. Through its self-reflexivity, parodying all types of representation, and through the use of irony, postmodern representation shows that all forms of culture—whether high art or popular culture, across various different media platforms—are grounded in ideology, and, therefore, cannot avoid their political contexts. In this sense, postmodern art, according to Hutcheon, is political through and through, at the very least in the sense that it acknowledges that its representations are never neutral. From Hutcheon, we can gather that at the heart of postmodernism and postmodern representations is a sense of self-consciousness, self-reflexivity, parody, and irony. Postmodernism, she says, differs from previous forms of cultural and literary criticism because of the kind of *self*-awareness that it presents. Modern art, for instance, saw culture as the source of representations, whereas postmodernism sees it as its effect. Although past forms of criticism have addressed expressive, mimetic, and formalist concerns, what makes postmodernism different is the degree of reflexivity it brings to these types of criticism. Furthermore, it is because of the impact of feminist, gay, lesbian, queer, Marxist, race, ethnicity, postcolonial, and post-structuralist theory that postmodern criticism adds a deeper social and political awareness to studies of the affective, representational/imitative, and formalist aspects of art and culture. Postmodern criticism therefore brings an added dimension of the interrogation of the ways that society, politics, and ideology shape meaning. Representations are now understood as a *product* of ideology, and likewise, *ideology is seen as a system of representation.*

Recognizing this, becoming self-aware, and being self-reflexive of the fact that our knowledge about the world comes pregnant with social and ideological meanings—that it never comes pure, from some neutral/objective place of understanding—is how postmodernism aims to dedoxify cultural representations. By raising representation as an issue, postmodernism aims to challenge our assumptions *about* representation. Postmodern art, according to Hutcheon, confronts both realist and formalist impulses in art. Modernism, she says, confronted realism in formalist terms. Postmodernism, however, is parodic about the confrontation between history and self-reflexivity. Self-reflexivity is, in this sense, a way of coming to terms with the manner in which narratives and images structure our conceptions of self and society. Parodic, ironic, self-reflexive postmodern art therefore enables a manner of deconstructing normative conventions within and across different forms of representation. Furthermore, unlike the high art of modernism and the avant-garde, postmodernism strives toward accessibility. Postmodernism also calls into question authoritative voices, *particularly western and patriarchal voices*, that underpin much of modern culture.

Through parody, irony, and self-reflexivity, postmodernism is able to both legitimize *and* subvert culture (both high culture and mass culture) at the same time. With this, Hutcheon challenges Jameson's claim about the loss of critical distance in postmodernism. Postmodern irony, according to Hutcheon, posits and then subverts critical distance.

Double-coding

Like Hutcheon, the architect, Charles Jencks defines the postmodern aesthetic as a process of "double-coding." Unlike Hutcheon, though, double-coding for Jencks does not imply the legitimization *and* the subversion of the dominant culture at one and the same time; rather, for him, double-coding involves the construction of a representation that is one part drawn from modern aesthetics and one part from elsewhere. Though the specific style varies from medium to medium in terms of its motivations and approaches, postmodern art and representation is generally, according to Jencks, a double-coded aesthetic: it is, he says, part modern and part traditional or local, enabling the kind of aesthetic populism that Jameson addresses, able to communicate with the public. It is a representation that is also one part the culture of the elite and one part populist, appealing to the masses who are the end users of the building. The problem with modern architecture, according to Jencks, was that it did not address the needs of its users. It also did not connect with its own location in the city, and with the city's history. Postmodern architecture, in contrast, is both professionally based *and* popular; it is also based on new techniques *and* old patterns. It is double-coded, then, in two ways: it is *both* elite *and* popular; and it is *both* new *and* old. Like Hutcheon, however, Jencks agrees that postmodernism makes use of irony, parody, displacement, complexity, eclecticism, and realism.

The motive for postmodernism, according to Jencks, is not necessarily the aesthetic failures of modern architecture; it is, rather, the *social* failure of modernism. To this extent, postmodernism appeals to the popular classes, or to its ultimate end users. It relies upon a populist aesthetic. Nevertheless, at the level of its elitism, postmodernism still faces and encounters the problem of deadlocks arrived at with limits to the new. Facing this problem, it therefore relies on ironic modes of presentation. Where everything has already been done, quotation again becomes part of the aesthetic of postmodern irony and parody. We see this in the lines cited by Jencks from Umberto Eco—where fearing a lack of originality, a man is not capable of saying to his lover directly, "I love you." He must express affect in a non-direct way, saying instead, "as a poet would have put it: I love you."[28] Because everything has already been said, novelty and originality prove difficult. Postmodern representation and aesthetics also appeal to a sense of pluralism, where the design must address various different tastes or taste cultures, and different views, making postmodern art quite eclectic as well.

Simulation, simulacra, and the hyperreal

To briefly summarize the account of postmodernism provided in the last few sections, what we can tell is that it is a style of presentation that holds a unique relationship with history in its manner of representation. Unique, I argue, because it is a relationship that dislodges the present from the past and the yet to come. Double-coding for Hutcheon and Jencks shows postmodernism to be highly self-reflexive, opting for ironic, parodic, and eclectic patterns of expression, which contemplate the past, announcing our awareness of it in the present, but ultimately incapable of moving beyond it. The lines from Umberto Eco exemplify this perfectly: the only way to come up with the new is through an ironic reference to what has already been done. I cannot say to my significant other, "I love you," because that is too cliché. All I can do is to cite the words that someone else has already said, to make my own words sound more original. But I claim that this makes the concept of pastiche all the more potent. Pastiche expresses a postmodern awareness of the past that actively loses its reference to the past. It presents the past as a stereotype of itself, without any recognition for its historical origins, and, therefore, despite the irony used in its presentation, still robs the reference of its context. It becomes a mere *simulation* or *simulacrum*—a copy without reference to the original—of the past. Yet, with the loss of history, constitutive of postmodernism, there is also an apparent loss of any reference to an underlying reality. This is viewed through the prism of the new electronic and digital media environment that the French media philosopher Jean Baudrillard refers to as "hyperreal."[29]

The hyperreal corresponds to the breakdown of the signifying chain, in the sense that here too a reference is lost: in this case, there is a loss to a deeper reality beneath the surface level of the representation. Since our environment is now permeated with simulations that precede the real thing, the hyperreal provides a sense of the kind of *surficial* atmosphere that characterizes the postmodern. For another example of how to imagine this kind of postmodern simulation, consider the sound effect of the click noise—the shutter noise—that is heard on a digital camera. The sound itself is unnecessary, but it mimics the mechanical sound of the shutter snapping on an analog film camera. The simulated effect is therefore purely superficial and affective. The filters used on Instagram are also exemplary, meant as they are to simulate the faded surfaces of polaroid photographs.

The hyperreal therefore bears a relation to the way that Jameson describes the waning of depth models, emphasizing the superficial level of appearances over essences. With its critical lens and suspicion for "essences" and "origins," which are seen as sources for fixing power and authority, postmodernism turns its attention to surfaces and appearances. This also provides an explanation for the postmodern attention to space over time: space is surficial; time adds depth, is often tied to some origin story, and is too teleological. Time and history also imply a subjective phenomenology, where there is a supposed *subject* of History, whereas space emphasizes overlapping multitudinous parallel discourses, without an identifiable (privileged) subject. "Hyperreality" thus also renders the "end of history" in the sense of doing away with the underlying need for essence and origin.

Implied in Baudrillard's conception of the hyperreal is a rejection of historical materialism, and the privilege assigned to the historical mode of production. In fact, postmodernism, for Baudrillard, signals the end of the era of production. In place of production as the organizing principle of society, postmodern culture, according to Baudrillard, is structured around digital media, informatics, cybernetics, and models of simulation. For Baudrillard, the postmodern represents a new mode of abstraction that emerged in the development of consumer society, alongside the rise of the new media spectacles of electronic media such as TV and computers. For Baudrillard, electronic media inform a new stage of abstraction, where all social relations become technologically mediated. Hyperreality therefore implies the dissolution of the boundary between image and reality, where the referent is lost. There is, in other words, no reality; there is only a hyperreal network of simulations, simulated in the new media environments of consumer spectacle.

Hyperreality, as a way of understanding representation, moves us away from an older distinction between reality and illusion, where the representation is a distortion of reality, where the representation hides a deeper reality, or where there exists an essence *below* the surface appearance. Now, the representation is *constitutive* of reality, particularly in the sense that there is no meaning of reality outside of the representation, not unlike the way that post-structuralists claim that there is no subject outside of discourse: reality is an *effect* of discourse or representation. In the sphere of art, too, all style, and all form has been exhausted. In this context, the only thing that art can do is to play around with the styles and genres already in existence. Therefore, it is only possible to *imitate* past novelty and style. This is how we might be able to understand versions of pastiche and parody in postmodern representations. But with hyperreality, simulations of past styles are given a new twist, appropriate for the age of the digital. Although "hyperreality" signals a loss of the reference to reality, behind the illusion it may however represent the manner in which de-historicized pastiche is tied together at a spatial, rhizomatic level. New media, in other words, can be the prism through which to view the postmodern appropriation of the past, and in this way becomes a sign of its double coding.

The postmodern subject

I have paid much attention above to questions about history, representation, and authority. Though implicit in these discussions, we must now turn more directly to a discussion of the postmodern subject. Modern subjectivity is perhaps best represented by the Cartesian *cogito*—René Descartes's "I think, therefore I am." The significance of this statement can be found most poignantly in the transition from premodern to modern times. The *cogito* provided legitimacy to the existence of a subject who is free from both God and the king. It was significant politically for providing a space in which the agency of the subject could be born to do away with the older powers of the *ancien regime*. But it is a notion of subjectivity that relies upon an image of a fully self-aware, centered individual: a conception that became central later on for bourgeois subjectivity, and the liberal conception of free agency. In modernism, therefore, we find representations of those feelings and affects that identify a loss of the sense of the centered ego of the subject. Feelings of anxiety and alienation predominate. This was then given further depth with Sigmund Freud's discovery of the unconscious and the mechanism of repression in his studies on hysteria.

The unconscious troubles the notion of a centered, self-aware ego, and posits the existence of a decentered element of the subject—a part of the subject, of which she is not fully aware. Hysteria, according to the Freudian interpretation, is the result of unwanted memories or feelings that the subject represses, but which then emerge as an hysterical symptom: a slip of tongue, a nervous tick, and so on. The unconscious is not simply just some deeper part of the self, access to which is difficult to locate, beneath the surface. It remains a part of ourselves that *is*, in fact, given expression in how we comport ourselves, how we speak and act; but it reflects an aspect of ourselves of which we are unaware. The modern subject is therefore caught in a nexus somewhere between the centered agency of the *cogito* and the decentered subjectivity of the unconscious and neurosis.

Modern subjectivity is also characterized by a liberal conception of human nature. The Western tradition of subjectivity, along with the centered agency of the *cogito*, sees the body as a primary component of our identity. This tradition finds its foundation in modern liberal political philosophy, in the work of thinkers often associated through their conception of a "state of nature" that preexisted civilized social relations and the "social contract." In the work of Thomas Hobbes, for instance, the state of nature is one of a "war of every man against every man." Men come together, according to Hobbes (and others such as John Locke and Jean-Jacques Rousseau) in order to create a bond that assures their mutual coexistence, making an agreement not to harm each other or each other's property. In this early modern liberal humanist conception of the natural self, there is a sense in which our identity is determined by the body—the human body.

According to the English philosopher John Locke, the state of nature is one of foundational equality, wherein every man has been given (by God) equality of mind *and* body. Every man has the physical ability to take of the earth, and the cognitive capabilities to know how to make good rational use of it, in order to satisfy *his* needs and wants. No man, he says, may take more than his fair share of the resources of the earth, an amount that would be noticeable in his taking so much that some of his property is left to spoil or rot, which would indicate an irrational use of the earth. To make his case, he describes the Aboriginal populations of the Americas as being rich in land but not enjoying all of the luxuries that the Europeans enjoy. For Locke, this is an indication that the "Americans," as he calls them, do not in fact have legal ownership over the land, a point that he uses in order to justify European colonialism. It should be noted, then, that the liberal humanist conception of subjectivity advanced by thinkers like Locke and Hobbes is indicative of an underlying Eurocentrism and sexism (the typical, or even ideal, subject is thought of unconsciously as white and male). Postmodernism posits a challenge to the liberal humanist conception of the subject, on both cognitive *and* corporeal levels.

Postmodernism posits two notions of the "death of the subject": on the one hand, there is an "historicist" version, which identifies the decentering of the autonomous bourgeois subject, or the liberal and Cartesian *cogito*, and the subject of the nuclear family—a decentering that would be impossible without the Freudian discovery of the unconscious and the mechanism of repression. On this account, the neurotic/hysteric describes the modern subject—the subject of the Oedipus complex, and what Deleuze and Guattari later refer to as the mommy-daddy-me triad. If, then, this version of the death of the subject posits merely its decentering, the post-structuralist conception, on the other hand, suggests that this subject never really existed in the first place, and that the modern notion of the subject is a mere illusion.

If the *cogito*-neurotic represents the modern subject, and the bourgeois subject of "classical" capitalism, then the schizophrenic, according to Deleuze and Guattari, represents the subject of late capitalism. Since, according to them, exchange relations in the market unhinge all fixed meanings, the schizo emerges as *the* subject of capitalism. Psychoanalysis, according to them, is therefore a repressive mechanism to re-hystericize the subject, bringing her back into the fold of the bourgeois and Oedipal psychic makeup. The postmodern subject is, on this account, *fragmented* rather than *alienated*, and postmodern criticism is instructed to fight any attempt to reinterpret or narrativize the subject back into its previously repressive/repressed position.[30]

Likewise, postmodernism challenges the liberal humanist conception of the "natural" human body, or the conception of "human" identity based upon the *determination* of the body. Not only in the sense of a "state of nature," but also—and against Freud's dictum that "biology is destiny"—that one's identity is determined by their genitals. Deleuze and Guattari, in *A Thousand Plateaus* (*Milles plateaus*, 1980), also claim that modern science and technology have had an affect/effect on how we conceive subjectivity. Cybernetic and informational technologies now create "human-machine systems."[31] Drawing on their work, Donna Haraway, in "A Cyborg Manifesto," argues that cyborg is today perhaps the best representation of postmodern subjectivity: a subject fabricated and organized as a hybrid between biological organisms and machines. The cyborg, she claims, allows us to reconceive the politics of the subject. Human agency, according to Haraway, is dependent upon our interaction with many nonhuman elements, including information and entertainment technologies, not to mention prosthetic devices that we attach to our bodies for our survival. Not only the disabled, but even those technologies that we use to make and create accessibility in our everyday lives, from the wearing of glasses and the use of automobiles for transportation, to the use of drugs and medication: prosthetics that allow us to control and manipulate our ever-changing environments. Cyborg theory therefore dismantles the liberal humanist conception of a "natural" self.

N. Katharine Hayles similarly provides a potent critique of liberal humanist conceptions of the subject, arguing instead that we are all now "posthuman." Posthumanism, as a critical concept, is meant to do away with the liberal notion of a natural self, but it also involves rejecting the underlying Eurocentrism and sexism *implied* in liberal humanism, which both feminism and postcolonial theory have been keen to address in the postmodern "culture wars." Posthumanism therefore conceives the construction of subjectivity as fragmented and based in human–machine interactions and networks.

Allegorical interpretation

Now that we have a more fully developed conception of the key characteristics of postmodernism; its approach to aesthetic populism; its critical approach to cultural representation through concepts like pastiche, double-coding, and the hyperreal; and the posthuman conception of the subject, I would like to address a final critical model that distinguishes postmodern from modern criticism. Symbolism, for modern critics, was an appropriate approach to interpretation, and one that allowed them to question the underlying meaning of the text. Since postmodernism rejects such a binary opposition between surface and depth, there has been a stronger turn toward allegorical interpretation.

Allegory, according to the postmodern critic Craig Owens, is a process of interpreting one text through the purview of another.[32] It is not a hermeneutic practice, where the interpretation is meant to reveal the truth of the text. Rather, allegory is a kind of *supplement* to the original text. It is a practice of rewriting the text using the terms of another, and in this way produces a wholly new meaning where the theory arrived at is the product of interaction between the two. For me at least, the postmodern practice of allegorical interpretation is one of its merits. Its goal is not to uncover the ultimately true meaning of the text in question. Instead, it makes use of the text as part of the process of "cognitive mapping," where we can make use of it—we can borrow from it—in order to further enhance our understanding of our present circumstances.

Postmodern artists are allegoricists as well, according to Owens. They generate their own meanings by borrowing from and referencing other texts; and, in this way, a new light is shed on the practice of pastiche. Like pastiche, Owens notes that postmodern art, in a kind of palimpsestitic fashion, draws upon images of the past, but without reference. Film styles or genres are exemplary here. "The western, the gangster saga, science fiction," he writes, "these are the allegories of the twentieth century."[33] Postmodernism quotes these styles, but without their specificity. Allegory, in this sense, is a self-reflexive process, and becomes a kind of "counter-narrative" that involves substituting—or rather, replacing—one text with another. However, Owens also claims that postmodernism signals a shift from historical to *discursive allegory*—discourses on race, gender, capitalism, art, the discourse of the signifier, psychoanalysis, and so on, all become parallel discourses with equal interpretive clout. In this respect he differs from Jameson, whose opening statement from *The Political Unconscious* (1981) commands theorists to "Always historicize!"

Jameson agrees that the allegorical interpretation is central to reading cultural objects. However, for him, history—or more specifically, historical materialism—is the master narrative according to which the text must be allegoricized. The shift from history to discourse therefore indicates a key difference between modernist and postmodernist allegorical processes. Or, as Jameson might put it differently, this signals a shift from history (or "historicity") to historicism, where the reference presented in the text loses its historical specificity and becomes recognizable or familiar, but without a reference to the historical past. In a way, this accounts for the centrality that postmodern art assigns to the spectator or reader.

As a reader, then, my objective is to take the postmodern allegorical impulse and apply it to a historical materialist reading of postmodernism. I claim that practices of pastiche, double-coding, irony, and simulation can only be understood in their full political capacity if they are read against the background of the commodity–class dynamics of contemporary capitalism. As we have seen, modernism first arose as a reactionary formation to developments taking place in the capitalist mode of production, and corollary transformations that emerged as part of the Enlightenment desire toward rationalization and institutionalization. The modern ethic of "make it new" drove the production of art, while it also drove the further development of modern capitalism. Seeking to distance itself from the logic of the market, modern artists carved out a space for themselves that they hoped would allow for the autonomous production of "art for art's sake." However, the capitalist imperative for total commodification, as well as the further institutionalization of modern art, transformed its practices of subversion, themselves, into the dominant ideology.

Postmodernism is what occurs when subversion is no longer subversive. There is a redoubling that occurs, where the new becomes impossible, and all that is left is a simulated reference to the past. The postmodern redoubling is also the product of an emergent political cynicism marked by the failure of the Left in the events of May '68, which has also impacted the theoretical discourse from early structuralism through screen theory and cultural studies, shifting attention away from the historical materialist theory of emancipation, and toward greater focus on issues of cultural representation. This has had the advantage of bringing greater attention to the critique of cultural stereotypes in modern texts, but it has also drained the desire for social and political transformation.

There have, then, been gains and losses with postmodern theory. Through commodification, the divide between high and popular culture becomes redundant, and commodified mass culture now becomes an object of art itself. In other words, the lines between art and commodity become meaningless. Binary logics between surface and depth, appearance and essence, also become suspect, since they would seem to support older Eurocentric and phallocentric conceptions of power. And with this, modern master narratives of history and subjectivity are taken as illusory, themselves supportive of older structures of power. With this in mind, my goal is to take up a postmodern practice of interrogation, but one that still sides with those older master narratives, in order to fully come to terms with the transformations that have taken place in postmodern capitalism. For me, historical materialism still proves useful for considering the ideology and context of postmodernism, and in a way that allows us to see past its cynical resignation. In order to accomplish this task, I use *Blade Runner* as an arm in my own practice of cognitive mapping.

Notes

1 See Roland Barthes, "The Death of the Author," in *Image-Music-Text*, trans. Stephen Heath (New York: Hill and Wang, 1977); and Michel Foucault, "What is an Author?" in *The Foucault Reader*, ed. Paul Rabinow (New York: Pantheon, 1984).

2 See Dick Hebdige, *Subculture: The Meaning of Style* (New York: Routledge, 2002).

3 Tim Robbins's mockumentary *Bob Roberts* (1992) plays upon this idea of the "rebel conservative," demonstrating precisely how postmodern practices of subversion can be easily appropriated by the Right.

4 See Marshall Berman, *All That Is Solid Melts Into Air: The Experience of Modernity* (New York: Penguin, 1982). Berman's text is essential reading for anyone interested in studying the dynamics of change and transformation brought forth by modernism and modern culture, and modernization as a political, economic, and technological force.

5 Jürgen Habermas, "Modernity—an Incomplete Project," in *The Anti-Aesthetic: Essays on Postmodern Culture*, ed. Hal Foster (New York: New Press, 1998).

6 My argument in this section relies on a thesis developed by Fredric Jameson in his article "Reification and Utopia in Mass Culture." *Social Text* 1 (1979): 130–48.

7 This is the claim made by Walter Benjamin in his well-known essay "The Work of Art in the Age of Mechanical Reproduction," in *Illuminations*, ed. Hannah Arendt (New York: Schocken, 1969).

8 For more on this, see John Berger, *Ways of Seeing* (New York: Penguin, 1972), especially the first chapter, which draws its inspiration from the Benjamin essay cited above.

9 Jameson, "Reification and Utopia," 134.

10 Clement Greenberg, "Avant-Garde and Kitsch," in *Art and Culture: Critical Essays* (Boston: Beacon Press, 1989).

11 See Max Horkheimer and Theodor Adorno, "The Culture Industry: Enlightenment as Mass Deception," in *Dialectic of Enlightenment*, trans. John Cumming (New York: Continuum, 1969).

12 The HBO series *Silicon Valley* (2013–present) dramatizes some of the ways in which the culture industry thesis is still operative in the information society, and in Web 2.0.

13 See Jean-Louis Comolli and Jean Narboni, "Cinema/Ideology/Criticism," in *Movies and Methods: An Anthology, Volume I*, ed. Bill Nichols (Berkeley: University of California Press, 1976). In his introduction to this piece, Bill Nichols notes that the objective of the authors, in the wake of the events of May '68, was to rethink the purpose of film criticism from a political standpoint in relation to Marxism, structural linguistics, and psychoanalysis.

14 I am hesitant to use the term "post-Structuralism," since this term was only popularized later on by American scholars writing and working with (mainly) French theorists critical of structuralism, but who never actually made use of the term itself. I am using it here, therefore, only to simplify and to show a historical shift between the two approaches.

15 For a deeper investigation of psychoanalytic film theory, its development in the "screen-theory" of the 1970s, and its more recent incarnations, see Todd McGowan, *Psychoanalytic Film Theory and the Rules of the Game* (New York: Bloomsbury, 2015), 56–70.

16 See Laura Mulvey, "Visual Pleasure and Narrative Cinema," in *Film Theory: An Anthology*, ed. Robert Stam and Toby Miller (Oxford: Wiley-Blackwell, 2000).

17 Francis Fukuyama, "The End of History?" *The National Interest* 16 (Summer 1989): 3–18; and *The End of History and the Last Man*. Reissue edition (New York: Free Press, 2006). It should be noted that Fukuyama later abandoned this thesis with the arrival of the Iraq war of 2002 and the financial crisis of 2008.

18 Fredric Jameson, "'End of Art' or 'End of History'?" in *The Cultural Turn: Selected Writings on the Postmodern, 1983–1998* (New York: Verso, 1998).

19 Foucault, "Truth and Power." In *The Foucault Reader*, 60.

20 Michel Foucault, "Nietzsche, Genealogy, History,"
in *The Foucault Reader*, ed. Paul Rabinow
(New York: Pantheon, 1984).

21 Gilles Deleuze and Felix Guattari, *Anti-Oedipus: Capitalism
and Schizophrenia*, trans. Robert Hurly, Mark Seem, and Helen
R. Lane (Minneapolis: University of Minnesota Press, 1983).

22 Slavoj Žižek, *The Ticklish Subject: The Absent Center of
Political Ontology* (New York: Verso, 1999).

23 Jameson, "Postmodernism," 53–92.

24 David Harvey, *The Condition of Postmodernity*
(Oxford: Blackwell, 1989), 59.

25 Raymond Williams, "Culture is Ordinary," in *On Culture &
Society: Essential Writings*, ed. Jim McGuigan (Thousand Oaks,
CA: Sage, 2013).

26 Jameson, "Postmodernism, or, the Cultural Logic of Late
Capitalism," 54.

27 Linda Hutcheon, *The Politics of Postmodernism* 2nd ed.
(New York: Routledge, 2002)

28 Charles Jencks, "Postmodern and Late Modern: The Essential
Definitions." *Chicago Review* 35.4 (1987): 37.

29 Jean Baudrillard, "The Precession of Simulacra," in *Simulacra
and Simulations*, ed. Sheila Faria Glaser (Ann Arbor: University
of Michigan Press, 1994).

30 Drawing on the work of Slavoj Žižek, particularly in *The Ticklish
Subject*, it could be argued that the problem with postmodern
subjectivity is that of *perversion* and not schizophrenia or
psychosis. Instead of the subjectivization found in the analytical
discourse, postmodern capitalism, and its constant injunction
to "Enjoy!" interpellates the subject in the mode of perversion,
a subjective position in which a figure of repressive authority is
demanded and willed into existence, a condition upon which the
subject is able to continue to follow her pleasures.

31 Gilles Deleuze and Felix Guattari, *A Thousand
Plateaus: Capitalism and Schizophrenia*, trans. Brian Massumi
(Minneapolis: University of Minnesota Press, 1987), 458.

32 Craig Owens, "The Allegorical Impulse: Toward a Theory of
Postmodernism." *October* 12 (1980): 67–86.

33 Craig Owens, "The Allegorical Impulse: Toward a Theory of
Postmodernism Part 2." *October* 13 (1980): 74.

CHAPTER TWO

Postmodernism and *Blade Runner*

Mapping the historical logic of *Blade Runner*

Blade Runner is a film that, depending upon the manner in which it is addressed, can be claimed by various critical perspectives and theoretical approaches. Perhaps it is this very fact that allows us to claim *Blade Runner* for postmodern critical theory. *Blade Runner* makes possible a kind of "cognitive mapping" of postmodernism as a historical, social, and political moment. As I argue in this chapter, it is the film's attention to history and subjectivity both formally and thematically, that allows us to view the film through the lens of postmodernism; but insofar as we read it allegorically, through the prism of historical materialism, *Blade Runner* also provides a cognitive mapping of our own context in contemporary capitalist society. In fact, the film is significant not only because it exemplifies the postmodern but also because it can be seen as a marker of the transition from modernity to postmodernity, from modernism to postmodernism; and, as we will see, is helpful also for conceptualizing the transition from postmodernism to capitalist realism.

My reading of *Blade Runner* also makes use of the postmodern practice of intertextual interpretation. Without seeking to uncover the one true meaning of the film, a practice that was tied to the modern reflection on the symbolism of the text, I prefer to view the film in its relation to other similar films. In this way, I combine a surficial reading of the film of this sort—one that ties it in with a network of other postmodern films—to a historical materialist interpretation of postmodernism. Allegory and intertextuality, therefore, combine modern and postmodern practices of interpretation. I will show, then, why *Blade Runner* is postmodern, but I will also use the film to reveal the *historicity* of postmodernism.

Not only do I read the film intertextually in relation to other films, I also look at the film in and across various media. By considering the changing viewing formats of the film and its various manifestations, from the original US Theatrical Release (1982), to the Director's Cut (1992), and the Final Cut (2007), from theatre to VHS to DVD and now online streaming, my analysis shows where form and content overlap in *Blade Runner*. The film is, in this sense, perhaps one of the clearest examples for believing in the continued relevance of postmodern theory—particularly in film studies and in film and cultural theory—matched, perhaps, by the *Star Wars* franchise. Signs of postmodernism are evident in both *Blade Runner* (1982) and *Star Wars* (1977) stylistically, and both have reappeared in recent years to mark their continuity with capitalist realism. In the case of *Star Wars*, I'm speaking not (only) of the prequel series (Episodes I–III), nor the new series of sequels (*The Force Awakens*), but also, and probably more significant, the technological transformations of the original film series (From *Star Wars* to *Return of the Jedi*).

It is a little-known fact that the original *Star Wars* film was adapted, once it was released on video cassette—the year after the release of *The Empire Strikes Back* (1980), to include in the opening crawl sequence the subtitle: "Episode IV: A New Hope."[1] This was done in order to build in continuity between the first film and the two that followed. *Empire* now became "Episode V," and *Return of the Jedi* (1983) became "Episode VI." Later on, as a prelude to the release of the prequel series, the original trilogy was released in 1997 as a series of "Special Editions," which contained new digitally enhanced effects, the addition of deleted scenes with new digital changes, and even a new digital musical sequence in Jabba the Hut's palace in *Return of the Jedi*. Following the release of the prequel series (1999–2005), the original trilogy was released on DVD with additional changes, most notably in the final sequence of *Jedi*, where Luke Skywalker looks on at the ghosts (or spirits) of Obi Wan Kenobi, Yoda, and Anakin Skywalker. In the original sequence, Anakin is played by the stage actor Sebastien Shaw; however, in the new DVD release of the film, the spirit of Anakin is played by Hayden Christensen, who stars as Anakin in the prequels. While on the one hand, replacing Shaw with Christensen creates a kind of seamless continuity between the prequels and the original series, on the other hand it is a further example of the formal evacuation of the film's history through the use of digital technology and effects. Its digital formalism concedes its "historicity." *Blade Runner* has its own similar experience.

Ridley Scott's film has gone through its own series of permutations, from the original cut to the 1992 Director's Cut, and more recently to the 2007 Final Cut of the film. In fact, seven distinct versions of the film are known to exist, five of which are included in the special 2012 Ultimate Collector's Edition of the film released on its thirtieth anniversary. These five include the original Workprint, the US Theatrical Release, the International Release, the Director's Cut (perhaps the most well-received and critically acclaimed version of the film), and the new Final Cut. The story about the completion of *Blade Runner* in its original US Theatrical Release version is now well known. The original Workprint version was screened for test audiences, who responded negatively to the film, following which the studio demanded significant changes. These changes included the addition of a longer opening background text providing context for the film, a longer voiceover narration provided by Deckard (Harrison Ford), and a happy ending sequence showing Deckard and Rachel driving away together. The Director's Cut differs in three significant ways from the original US Theatrical Release: (1) The voiceover narration is removed; (2) The "happy ending" sequence is removed; and (3) an additional short dream sequence is added of a unicorn running through a forest. This last addition, along with the removal of the happy ending sequence, has important ramifications (as I discuss below) for the ending and meaning of the film. The Final Cut, then, includes, in the only version of the film in which Scott had full creative control, scenes taken from the International Cut, which were included neither in the original US Theatrical Release, nor the 1992 Director's Cut, and newly discovered alternate shots with different angles of Deckard as he plays the piano in the famous daydream scene, spliced together with the unicorn sequence. The Final Cut has also been digitally enhanced, and includes reshot sequences.

Why is it worth addressing these changes to *Blade Runner*? Though they appear to provide a more beautiful cut of the film, and possibly bring enjoyment back to an older film, they also create something new. But what is new here is made possible by an evacuation of the past—of history. This, as we have seen, is what can be read as postmodern. At a formal level, the shift from *Blade Runner* (1982) to *Blade Runner: The Final Cut* (2007) highlights the shift from postmodernism to capitalist realism. If the original film was stylistically an example of pastiche, the Final Cut (not unlike the new *Star Wars* film, *The Force Awakens*) is a parody of the original—it removes the reference to history, on the one hand, stylistically through pastiche, while on the other hand locating its own history through the different versions of the film. It is also exemplary of the technological side of the postmodern relationship to history. The digital, as we have seen, manages to "spatialize" time—in the case of *Blade Runner*, this means the constant redux of the film, so that we can never really say that the most recent incarnation is the final version. Like our experiences of the debt and finance economy, *Blade Runner* is perpetually present.

Blade Runner also shows just where modernism and post-modernism begin to diverge.[2] While its themes elegize modernist conceptions of time, history, and memory, particularly through the portrayal of its main characters, its mise-en-scène celebrates the heterogeneity of postmodern hyperspace, simulation, spectacle, and pastiche. The film's attention to media and technology also reflects the postmodern evisceration of history, and the spatialization of time. Thematically, the film addresses issues of corporate elitism and the networks of multinational capital; it decenters the subject by questioning modern, liberal, and bourgeois conceptions of the centered subject of experience, and draws attention to the operations of time, duration, and memory as part of our centered experiences of selfhood, but it also forces reflection upon those qualities that constitute the human, or more specifically, liberal humanism and "human nature." The film is cluttered with glossy images of consumer spectacle, digital technology, video screens, video phones, and computer monitors, but it also displays decay, and a cultural density that makes it difficult to distinguish a particular aesthetic style, or even a specific locale (though we are told at the outset that the film takes place in Los Angeles).

Its visual style is a hybrid, made up of citation, quotation, reference, and pastiche. It takes place in the future (more so for its original audience in 1982 than for us in the second decade of the twenty-first century), but it is a future that is recognizable in its reference to stereotypes of past styles. The costumes worn by the characters and the fashion of the film reference the film noir of the 1940s, but also the punk rock of the 1970s and early 1980s. The architecture and design of the city are a mix of gothic and art deco, but also contain references to the pyramids of ancient Egypt, or the Mayan and Aztec pyramids of southern Mexico. Brand logos adorn the sides of buildings—Pan Am and Coca-Cola advertisements flash from the video screens that make up the city's skyline. If this is the future, then it is one that is still eerily familiar, plagued by the cluttered spectacle of consumer society. The film, then, does seem to border between themes of high modernism and the emerging postmodern culture of late capitalism (emerging, that is to say, in 1982, but full blown for us, today—more on this below). But if we consider how the film has been changed and transformed across various viewing platforms, from novel and its adaptation as a film to its release on VHS, its reincarnation as the Director's Cut, and then the Final Cut on DVD, it is possible to position the film as postmodern in another way.

A simulacrum of itself

The plot of *Blade Runner* varies in both minor and significant ways, depending on which version or format of the film we are watching. The film is based loosely on Philip K. Dick's novel, *Do Androids Dream of Electric Sheep?* (1968), and in the kind of translation that it presents, *Blade Runner* says something about the postmodern practices of film adaptation. *Blade Runner* adopts many elements from the novel, but is not a direct adaptation, much in the same way that Terry Gilliam's *Twelve Monkeys* 1995), was "inspired" by Chris Marker's short film *La Jetée* (1962). It borrows from the original thematically, but is not itself a replica. It is, in this way, a simulacrum of the novel—a copy without an original.

Blade Runner reproduces from the novel representations of a high-tech society, and qualities of paranoia and schizophrenia embodied in its main characters. The film, like the novel, takes place in the not-too-distant future, in November of 2019, and is set in a postapocalyptic Los Angeles, California. But "adaptation" becomes a tricky word, too, when we consider the various incarnations of the film. These incarnations help to develop the film's relationship to history (both its own and that of the postmodern). As I maintain, the Final Cut of the film, as the "preferred version," troubles the status of the previous versions. Were they simply a matter of "dress rehearsal"? First and second "drafts" or "editions" of the film? Or was there something particular to each version in relation to their medium and manner of exhibition or viewing? In other words, was the original US Theatrical Release specific to that time and viewing space, just as the Final Cut is now specific to spectatorship on the screen of the smart TV or tablet?

Although the film did poorly at the box office, opening in June of 1982, competing against other sci-fi and action blockbusters—notably Steven Spielberg's *E.T.: The Extra Terrestrial*, Steven Lisberger's *Tron*, and Nicholas Meyer's *Star Trek II: The Wrath of Khan*—it later received throughout the 1980s a strong cult following. The poor initial response is often charged to disparities between the film itself and its marketing, with previews that showed more of the action sequences and shots of the high-tech city. Critics and viewers had complained that the story was slow and confusing, and not the fast paced sci-fi-action film they were promised by the previews. In subsequent years, midnight screenings of the film led to renewed interest. Around 1990–1991, pirated versions of the Workprint began to circulate, and Warner Bros. started screening it in select theatres in Los Angeles and San Francisco.

The Workprint version is the original cut of the film shown to test audiences prior to the original US Theatrical Release. It received negative reviews and the film was subsequently changed in key areas for the theatrical release. The voiceover narration of Deckard providing expository elements of the story was added on, as was the "happy ending" of Deckard and Rachael driving off into the natural setting. The Workprint also didn't include the opening title sequence that explains the background of the replicants and blade runners. Instead, it includes a 2016 dictionary definition of "Replicant." Another version of the film, the International Theatrical Release, was later released in North America on VHS and laser disc as the "10th Anniversary Edition," and includes longer violent action sequences, which were also later included in the Final Cut.

These details are worth noting since we can see that, in part, the historical development of the film has been dependent upon factors beyond the scope of the film itself, and are a product of its time and place. This is not unique to *Blade Runner*, but as we can see, the political economy of the film industry—as a culture industry—has had a role in shaping the format of the film. From the Workprint to the US Theatrical Release, the aesthetic, form, and narrative of the film were determined by expectations about the audience, as were the poor box office returns for the initial release of the film determined by audience expectations of the film, based on marketing and competition. Film, unlike other media, is therefore much more overdetermined by market factors. On the one hand, this exemplifies the Frankfurt School concerns with the culture industry and mass culture; on the other hand, however, the cult around *Blade Runner* has also demonstrated clearly how high art and popular culture fold into each other in postmodernism.

Because of the popularity of the Workprint, and the growing cult status of the film throughout the 1980s, Warner decided to produce an official Director's Cut of the film.[3] The latter is arguably the most widely appreciated by viewers, critically acclaimed, and discussed version of the film, owing perhaps to the ambiguity surrounding Deckard, but also because it more strongly upholds the generic, visual, and formal language set out by the rest of the film. In other words, part of the problem with the original US Theatrical Release was the incongruity between its formal style and the meaning provided by the original conclusion to the film. The Director's Cut seemed to have corrected this problem, but the outcome was a wholly new meaning produced by the film.

Apart from dropping the tacked-on "happy ending" sequence at the film's conclusion, and the voiceover narration, the Director's Cut is noted for adding a significant amount of intrigue into the film, focused mainly on the ambiguity of whether or not Deckard is a replicant. About halfway through the Director's Cut, a new scene appears, spliced into an already existing scene of Deckard sitting in his bathrobe, somberly playing a few keys on the piano, looking at the portraits that sit atop. This new scene shows a unicorn running through a forest, and it is apparent that this is an image that Deckard sees in a dream (or daydream, since he is not sleeping). The addition of this scene is important since it completely changes the film's ending and meaning, and shows quite significantly the importance of film editing in its production of meaning. When Deckard finds the origami unicorn left by Gaff at the end of the film, this can be read as a sign that Deckard is not human, after all. Now, the film forces us to ask: Is Deckard a replicant?

From *Electric Sheep?* to *The Final Cut*, *Blade Runner* is inherently a product of postmodernity, a constant simulacrum of itself. It is impossible to say that any one version is more authentic than the others; it is also difficult to say which one is truly the "original." And, in this way, the film drops the concern for origins, or essences, tied to the postmodern critique of master narratives. The original US Theatrical Release is itself an adaptation of the novel, though it is not a direct replication, and many details are changed or added in the film that were not part of the novel. Even the title of the film is taken from another story. Though based on Dick's novel, the film's title is taken from that of the short story written by William S. Burroughs, *Blade Runner: A Movie* (1979). Burroughs's short story was never turned into a movie, and the term was bought to be used to describe Deckard's job and for the title of Scott's film.

The Director's Cut, then, reflects Scott's original intentions with the film, but is overturned by the release of the Final Cut, which, Scott says, is his preferred version of the film. Though it is "preferred," the Final Cut is not the first version and much more difficult to claim as first in line. But can the preferred intention and vision also count as original at a conceptual level? If the Final Cut is the product that was originally intended, can we say that all of the other versions are retroactively secondary? In this sense, *Blade Runner* is always a simulacrum of itself, with each version marking and adding a new layer to the historicity of its form. The "original" version seems to matter less and less.

The different versions of *Blade Runner* are also worth considering at the formal level of digital cinema. What both

Blade Runner and *Star Wars* show us is that, with digital cinema, cinema can be rethought as a new practice of visual art as animation, where live action is but one component of its overall form.[4] *Blade Runner: The Final Cut* takes elements of the original film and transforms them into something new. It is, in this way, not unlike writing on a digital document (as opposed to the typewriter). With the digital document, writing never really ends. You can easily delete, copy and paste, revise, and rewrite with minimal cost, whereas with the old typewriter, it was more difficult to erase and delete, edit, and refashion the same work. With the computer, apparently just as with digital cinema, there is never any end to the work.[5] In this way, too, the film is infinitely a work in progress, still caught in a perpetual present.

While the newer versions of the film can be seen as newer and newer simulations of the original, the film can also be seen as simulacra in a much more widely acknowledged way. One of the most agreed upon dimensions of the film that allow us to claim it as postmodern is its play with the generic conventions of modern cinema. Through its use of past generic styles, *Blade Runner* is a simulacrum of past genres in film, exemplary of what we have already discussed as "pastiche."

Nostalgia and pastiche

Pastiche is like history folding in on itself; folding in because it is a product of the subtraction of the new. If modernism was defined by the constant production of the "new," postmodernism is what happens when there is nothing uniquely new to produce. The modern quest for novelty reaches its limit with postmodernism. Now it is certainly questionable whether the "newness" of the modern "new" was really very new in the first place. Original, unique, authentic—these are propositions that a postmodern critique of modernism shows to be fallacious, or, at least, it tries to make this case, suggesting that claims about originality, uniqueness, and authenticity are demonstrative of a fixing authority or power that underlies their assertions. In any case, at the level of style, postmodern pastiche may be thought of in terms of a turning back against the "newness" of modern style itself. We see this particularly in the aesthetics of postmodernism, which cite and refer to modern aesthetics and genres.

Through citation and reference of the past in modernism, postmodernism can be said to be either depriving us of history, or parodying history ironically, aiming to dedoxify the original. Depriving us of history, that is, by eliminating the historical *referent* to the style and aesthetic, itself. Postmodernism can be seen as parody, in contrast, because the reference or citation can be said to be speaking to a savvy audience, one that finds it recognizable, and is capable of understanding the irony in its operationalization, even recognizing the critique of ideology that is present in its form. In either case, an exact reference to the original is lacking, but whether or not this historical original is implicit is a matter of debate. Regardless of whether or not the referent is present, postmodernism certainly does combine elements, at least, of the past—past styles, genres, looks, and so on, and by combining citations to different styles it might be said to be producing something, if not new, then at least different from modernism. In this sense, postmodernism might not necessarily reflect a definitive break from modernism; however, it does signal a re-presentation of the meaning of modern signifiers. Again, modern genres become postmodern codes. In the realm of cinema, we need only consider the play with genre that has been used to classify many popular films as "postmodern."

Pastiche is tied to the postmodern sensibilities and memories of the mass culture of the past, where films about or set in the past, such as George Lucas's *American Graffiti* (1973), or Roman Polanski's *Chinatown* (1974), are less direct representations of the past than they are representations of the *cultural stereotypes* of the past.[6] Why refer to these films as "pastiche" instead of some other category of historical film? Consider a film like *Star Wars* (1977), which for Jameson exemplifies the similarities of pastiche shared by all three films. *Star Wars*, like *American Graffiti* and *Chinatown*, is an example of what he refers to as "nostalgia films." *Star Wars*, though not set in our own past—it is, however, set "a long time ago, in a galaxy far far away ...," as the opening titles of the film indicate—still recalls at the level of its formal detail, 1930s radio, and 1950s television adventure serials. Steven Spielberg's *Raiders of the Lost Ark* (1980) is similar in this regard. Though it *is*, like *American Graffiti* and *Chinatown*, set in the past, it is a representation of *cultural stereotypes of the past* and past styles, found for instance, in adventure novels and comic strips. Instead of parodying these styles, according to Jameson—and in contrast to someone like Linda Hutcheon—they rather satisfy a repressed desire to once again experience them.

To understand the difference between Jameson's claim about pastiche and Hutcheon's arguments about parody, we might look at the differences between Gary Ross's *Pleasantville* (1998) and Peter Weir's *The Truman Show* (1998). Both films, released in the same year, reference past generic styles of the *Leave it to Beaver* or *Father Knows Best* family television series of 1950s. *Pleasantville*, though, is less ironic in its presentation of the cultural stereotype of the series about the small town patriarchal family. It uses this convention in order to make a historical claim about personal-psychological, as well as sexual progress in American culture. As the self-actualization of characters occurs through sexual liberation, the film is colorized: the characters turn from black and white into color. The entire film is colorized once the cultural politics of the film's plot move from the conservative 1950s into the liberal 1960s—we even see more African American characters in the background as opposed to the mainly white characters seen throughout most of the film. *Pleasantville* uses the formal technique of colorization to play around with the genre, and to express its own political self-awareness. It also relies upon a kind of nostalgia of cultural stereotypes of 1950s television series and the historical shift toward political and sexual liberation in the

1960s—in part, a reference to that period of postwar transition in the welfare state period and the rise of the new social movements.

The Truman Show, however, is closer to Hutcheon's conception of postmodern parody. The film *is* ironic in its reference to the idyllic small-town patriarchal family of TV's yesteryear. Like *Pleasantville* it calls for a kind of liberation from this more conservative setting. But rather than reference the past style, *The Truman Show* uses comedy to parody these conventions, even alerting us to the off-camera cultural construction of the show itself in the film. In both films, characters are on or *in* the television. In *Pleasantville*, the two siblings are zapped into the TV; in *The Truman Show*, Truman is a character on TV. While *Pleasantville* uses this device to reference the past, and in conservative Fukuyamaist fashion, signals the "end of history" (the characters find liberation not in their own personal circumstances in the present, but by returning the site of past struggles), *The Truman Show* claims this device as an object of parody. It does this, though, usefully, as a model of postmodern ideology critique of the political economy of the media, the culture industry, and the cult of celebrity.

Other filmmakers, like Quentin Tarantino, tap into this style of deploying past cultural stereotypes, playing with and assembling a mix of genres—or rather, breaking down generic barriers from the modern period of mass culture. Films like *Pulp Fiction* (1994) and *Kill Bill Vol. 1* (2003) and *Kill Bill Vol. 2* (2004), blend stereotypical styles and conventions from gangster and crime films, the so-called Grindhouse films of the 1970s, comedy, noir, the revenge film, Samurai films, and Westerns. Tarantino's films also manipulate time, creating asynchronous plots with nonlinear stories, a technique used in other postmodern films, like Christopher Nolan's *Memento* (2000), in which the story unfolds in reverse—the first scene in the plot is in fact the final chronological scene in the story. The result is a flattening out of time, with priority given to the surface level of the style and the pastiche of generic conventions.

The effect, as Jameson puts it, is a nostalgic feeling—nostalgia for the past styles, represented through the cultural stereotypes that they've become.

A noir sci-fi

Blade Runner is a prime example of postmodern pastiche, overlapping as it does generic conventions of sci-fi and film noir. Combining references to each while responding to postmodern themes, particularly the technological and imagery of the digital, the cybernetic, and the network, has helped to place it within the postmodern sci-fi subgenre of "cyberpunk." It is through pastiche that we can begin to historicize *Blade Runner* at a formal level. By looking at the way the film mixes conventions from film noir and sci-fi, we can see precisely how the film simulates conventions from past genres while still removing references to them in their historical origin, not unlike Cindy Sherman's film stills. Therefore, by discussing genre and pastiche in *Blade Runner* we can come to an understanding of how postmodernism relates to—or, as Owens puts it, allegorizes—history.

At the first approach, *Blade Runner* is evidently an example of sci-fi. But critics have noted, as well, the fact that it references and borrows narrative and stylistic conventions from film noir. The darkness of the film, its use of space, its mise-en-scène, and use of light and shadow—its chiaroscuro lighting—are all reminiscent of '40s noir cinema. But its set and production design are even a little more eclectic than that. Gothic architecture and expressionistic use of shadow and perspective, particularly in its portrayal of the urban landscape, at times make the Los Angeles of *Blade Runner* look more like the Gotham City of Tim Burton's *Batman* (1989). This technique for representing the city still adds to the affective level of noir cinema by creating the appearance of a dark and ominous setting.

The film's set and production designs also contain an aesthetic that I would call (for lack of a better term) "digital." The walls of the pyramids making up the buildings of the Tyrell

Corporation and the rooftop of the police station and other buildings are coated with wires and circuits resembling the motherboard of a computer or a computer chip. High above ground, the space traversed by the hover cars is walled by digital displays, high gloss spectacle, and the neon lighting of advertising and branding, both of the image of the Coca-Cola advertisement that Deckard and Gaff travel past on their way to the Tyrell building, and the advertisement for the Off-World colonies, seen at various moments in the film.

Fashion and costume design are also elementary components of the film's noir and sci-fi aesthetics, with Rachael and Deckard adorning styles reminiscent of the '40s noir, while Roy Batty and Pris adopt punk styles seen elsewhere in the densely diverse crowd on the streets of this dystopian Los Angeles. The film is also marked by a neo-orientalism, fashioned in the portrayal of a few minor characters, such as the Asian food-stand owner, the eye manufacturer, Hannibal Chew, and the Egyptian manufacturer of the synthetic snake, Abdul Ben-Hassan. The metropolitan look of the city is made to resemble Tokyo or New York, much more so than Los Angeles, and the effect is the production of a space that is both totalizing and claustrophobic. It is a space that is an everywhere and a nowhere—a kind of "heterotopia." But it is also a space that puts on display the negative self-image of an enterprising modernism. The Los Angeles of *Blade Runner* is made to resemble the dark underside of the modern drive toward development gone wrong.

The narrative and plot of *Blade Runner* are also highly reminiscent of noir plots, like Carol Reed's *The Third Man* (1949), Billy Wilder's *Double Indemnity* (1944), and Howard Hawks's *The Big Sleep* (1946). Typically, these are films about a lone hero, usually some kind of detective or investigator, who, through his line of work, encounters a woman—the so-called femme fatale—who is often mysterious, highly sexualized and seductive, and who becomes either the instigator of his demise or, paradoxically, of his redemption. There is usually an element of sexual attraction or desire between the hero and the femme fatale, even if this does not actually result in sex between the characters. A femme fatale is generally a woman who does not conform to the conservative image of a devoted wife/mother of a nuclear family. She is typically without children, and, if married, seems distant with or even despising of her husband. The femme fatale often feels trapped by her husband or some other male figure and, though largely independent, seeks help or assistance from the male hero.

Noir films take place in cities, which are portrayed as vile and evil places where people are sinful and untrustworthy, and as abounding in crime. The hero is usually pitted against some corrupt authority figure and, through this antagonism, becomes the moral center of the film. There is a kind of "American" quality in film noir, partly because these were films made in the United States during the interwar period, and also because they are representative of American isolationism, forced to act as the moral compass of the dark and cruel world entering the war. Stylistically, film noir is generally characterized by low-key/chiaroscuro lighting, claustrophobic framing, shadows, unbalanced composition, and great depth of field. The hero usually wears a trench coat and a fedora, while the femme fatale typically wears darker clothing. Another prototypical feature of film noir is the use of a voiceover narrative, where the hero recounts the story in the first person. All of these characteristics and conventions—the femme fatale, the fedora- and trenchcoat-wearing detective, chiaroscuro lighting, voiceover narration—have now become some of the most recognizable stereotypes of film noir.

Blade Runner adopts signs of film noir in its style, costume design, mise-en-scène, lighting, and narrative structure. Deckard embodies the figure of the hard-boiled detective (or rather, he is the simulacrum of the noir detective), pulled back in after having quit his job through blackmail from Bryant. His outfit resembles that of the typical noir hero, wearing as he does a long trench coat, and the voiceover narration in the original US Theatrical Release rounds out and completes this persona in the film. In the process of his investigation, he meets

Rachael, here a simulacrum of the noir femme fatale. Through her mannerisms and dress, Rachael resembles the femme fatale of the '40s noir—the way she walks and speaks, the way that she smokes her cigarette while being interrogated by Deckard using the Voight-Kampff machine, her tight-fitting clothing with padded shoulders, her black feathered coat, her hairdo, are all component parts of her character's appeal. Sean Young portrays the character, initially as mysterious, alluring, and sexually sophisticated, though in the end she is played as much more vulnerable upon discovering the truth of her identity. She later seeks out Deckard, not directly for protection or for help with an investigation but in order to prove her innocence, in a manner of speaking. As a replicant, she is deemed an illegal, and therefore, upon being discovered by Deckard, she becomes a fugitive, a fact indicated about halfway through the film, after Deckard "retires" Zhora, and Bryant reminds him that he must retire Rachael, too.

Low-key lighting is used throughout the film, most evidently in Bryant's office, in the conference room at Tyrell's office where Rachael is interrogated, in the employee room where Holden interrogates Leon at the beginning of the film, and in Deckard's apartment. The film mixes claustrophobic interiors with open exteriors of the urban landscape. Apart from the scene where Deckard first arrives at the Tyrell Corporation where he meets Rachael, and we see a bit of sunlight from the setting sun—Deckard in fact asks Tyrell to dim the lights to help him administer the test—the city appears to be constantly dark, and it is often raining and wet. Very little is visible in Deckard's apartment, and the only light appears to be coming from windows leading outside and from small slits in the window blinds. However, from the claustrophobic interior of his apartment, we move to an equally suffocating depiction of the dark city as Deckard at one point goes out onto his balcony to look at the city streets below. We might expect the city outside to look more open, but the daunting architecture outside also creates a feeling of entrapment. The brightest scene in the film comes at the end of the original US Theatrical Release when

Deckard and Rachael travel north, making this last scene seem incongruous with the rest of the film's aesthetic.

If the world of *Blade Runner* is cruel and immoral, portrayed through noir conventions, it is the sci-fi conventions that bring forth a conflicting (perhaps even contradictory) morality. Science fiction films are typically moral tales. They are often films set in the future—at times this may be the distant future, as in the case of *Star Trek*, which takes place some three hundred to four hundred years from the twentieth and twenty-first centuries, or they may take place in the not-too-distant future, in films such as *Blade Runner*. The fact that sci-fi films are set in the future allows the audience to reflect upon the present from a moral standpoint. Is the future depicted, for instance, utopian or dystopian? More often than not it is the latter and the moral standpoint of the film reflects the question: Do we stay the course of our present society—will diverting from the present form of society, ideology, politics, and so on, bring forth a more dystopian society? Or, will not changing the present state of things result in a more dystopian future? Often, technology is presented as a major factor in the moral decay of the future society in sci-fi films; in other instances, technology is combined with corrupt forms of government, as in the literary example of George Orwell's *1984*. In some cases, corruption is the result of new, technologically and biologically determined forms of class inequality and oppression, as in Aldous Huxley's *Brave New World*, or in the film *Gattaca* (Andrew Niccol, 1997).

Sci-fi deals heavily with the technological, and its moral standpoint tends to reflect the role of technology in *human* society. Is our dependence on technology useful, that is, does it help to advance the human condition? Does it help to facilitate the lives of individuals and society? Or will our overdependence on technology result in the demise of our "humanity"? Some examples of sci-fi opt to depict the technological over and above the depiction of the future, for instance in Robert Zemeckis's *Back to the Future* (1985), where the young Marty McFly uses the Delorean time machine to travel back in time thirty years, when his parents were teenagers. The moral (and hypothetical) question posed by the film is whether or not we are justified in making changes to the past in order to improve our own conditions in the present.[7] The hypothetical problem of altering the (historical) timeline can be likened to the actual problem of geo-politics—of whether or not it is moral to affect or alter a local culture/society in the interests of another, as in the case of colonialism and imperialism. The television series *Star Trek: The Next Generation* (1987–1994), often deals with issues such as these, adopting in law the liberal "Prime Directive," including a "Temporal Prime Directive," creating rules around ambiguities in time travel. The Temporal Prime Directive is a historical counterpart, perhaps, to liberal multi-culturalism and its cultural relativism.

The question concerning technology, then (to borrow from the title of the well-known essay by Martin Heidegger), in the tradition of stories like Mary Shelley's 1818 novel *Frankenstein*, also adds to sci-fi a dimension regarding the morality of technology and (human) life. Or, more specifically, it asks the question: What *is* life? More on this below, but it is worth mentioning here since the narrative about the replicants in *Blade Runner*, and the questions it poses about the relation-ship between the technological and the biological, is one of the primary conventions of sci-fi dealt with in the film.

Blade Runner is recognizable as a sci-fi film, then, for a few different reasons. For one thing, it is set in the not-too-distant future of the year 2019. Thematically, the story deals quite substantially with the morality of creating artificial intelligence in the form of the replicants. More than that, it asks moral questions about how to treat artificial lifeforms—going even further in questioning the definition of life. Pris, speaking to Sebastien cites Descartes's "I think, therefore I am." What does it mean to "retire"—to kill—a replicant? Is this murder? Or simply the shutting off of a machine?

Visually, the film depicts technology in a way that has become typical of most sci-fi films. We see flying cars/hover-crafts throughout the film. The retrofitted cityscape flashes in neon and emulates what we might imagine the future to look like—at least, that is, from the perspective of the early 1980s, when the film was first shot. Technology also plays a key role in interrogating the replicants—the Voight-Kampff test is demonstrative of the fact that in this world, technology is still a tool used to "fight" technology.

Blade Runner is a dystopian film, but much of the dystopian elements of the film are set within the noir conventions discussed above. In fact, because the film draws upon elements of both noir and sci-fi, we can recognize here too an important dimension of postmodernism, which includes the attempt to keep open and unresolved any kind of conflict or contradiction. By combining noir—a genre that centers on the irresolvability of the immoral—with sci-fi—a genre couched in specifically moral terms—the film leaves open the tensions brought about by each genre as separate. Noir and sci-fi are part of a binary opposition of moral/immoral. They are contradictory, but like Jacques Derrida's practice of deconstruction, which looks at the relationship between binary opposites, where one of the terms comes to dominate the other (as in the binary between masculine and feminine, or between speech and writing), the contradiction remains unresolved. This is one way the film avoids the temporality—the time dimension—of becoming (change and transformation through resolution of the contradiction) in favor of the spatial dimension of simultaneous and fragmented being. Without a resolution to the contradiction, where neither point in the opposition is negated, the dialectical progression remains at a standstill. Unlike the Faustian desire for development that characterized modernity, neither the old nor the new, here, sublates the other. In fact, the simultaneity of noir and sci-fi depicts a movement that is both backward looking and forward looking at the same time. The film seems to suggest that the more we envision the future, the more we are inclined to encounter the past.[8] By combining stereotypical images of the past—and even past stereotypes about conceptions of the future—*Blade Runner* is a film that maintains an ambiguous relationship to time and history; and, this, as we can tell, signifies something about our own postmodern inability to locate ourselves in time and space. Nevertheless, for some critics, this space of the irresolvable tension of the immoral and moral—and our inability to locate ourselves in the time and space of the digital—is part of what defines the postmodern sci-fi subgenre of cyberpunk.[9]

Cyberpunk

Films like *Blade Runner*, David Cronenberg's *Videodrome* (1983), and Steven Lisberger's *Tron* (1982) are some of the earliest progenitors of the cyberpunk genre in film, but later incarnations include Brett Leonard's *The Lawnmower Man* (1992), Iain Softley's *Hackers* (1995), Robert Longo's *Johnny Mnemonic* (1995), Josef Rusnak's *The Thirteenth Floor* (1999), and of course, the Wachowski sisters' *The Matrix* (1999). The term itself derives from William Gibson's *Neuromancer* (1984), and his coinage of "cyberspace." Cyberpunk is a description, then, applied retroactively to films like *Blade Runner*, but with reference to it, used to describe films modeled after its own aesthetic later on. Though it can be regarded as the progenitor of the genre, many other films have modeled their aesthetic in part upon elements taken from *Blade Runner*. These include the street level of the Martian world in Paul Verhoeven's *Total Recall* (1990), and the dark streets of Coruscant in *Star Wars— Episode II: Attack of the Clones* (2002). Though the former, I would argue, is a good example of postmodern cinema— as are many of Verhoeven's films, particularly *Basic Instinct* (1992), a neo-noir film reminiscent of Lawrence Kasdan's *Body Heat* (1981), which is itself often claimed as one of the first initial examples of postmodernism in popular cinema, a pastiche of the older noir—the latter, unlike the original *Star Wars* (1977), is not. Or, to be more specific, the depiction of the dark streets of Coruscant, and particularly the bar scene where Obi Wan and Anakin search for the assassin, Zam Wesell, are a simulacrum of the scene in Taffy Lewis's bar in *Blade Runner*, as is the scene at the beginning of *The Matrix*, where Neo follows the "white rabbit" to the bar, where he meets Trinity.

The dark streets are important. Typically, Cyberpunk stories bring the spectator down from the top level of bureaucratic or big society imagery and conundrums, typical of traditional sci-fi, to the street level, which is much closer to the darker world of noir. But, unlike noir, the antagonist is less some individual acting out of strictly personal desire for power. In Cyberpunk, the enemy or villain is often a representative of big corporate power. In *Blade Runner*, this is portrayed in the character of Eldon Tyrell and the Tyrell Corporation. Cyberpunk is visually, as well, a retrofitted environment; sets are designed by tacking on the new—technologically—to the old. In *Blade Runner*, there exists still a palimpsest of older and newer signs of branding and advertising, the giant Coca-Cola advertisement on the digital display screen, viewed as the hovercraft carrying Deckard and Gaff flies by. The visual culture of this world is dominated by signs of corporate and commercial power. It is also a world that identifies visually the spatial distinction between the urban and the suburban, mainly through the advertisements for the Off-World colonies. There is a world "out there" in the film, but unlike sci-fi films like *Alien* (1979) or *2001: A Space Odyssey* (1968), where the action takes place mainly inside an enclosed spaceship somewhere in outer space, in *Blade Runner* the action takes place here, on Earth.

Blade Runner draws its influence not only from noir and sci-fi in cinema. Scott and his set designer Syd Mead also notably drew upon the adult comic book *Heavy Metal*, and its artists, including Moebius (the pseudonym used by the French artist Jean Giraud), Philippe Druillet, and Angus McKie. These artists, and their work in *Heavy Metal*, are noted for their depiction of a scaled, dark, and dense urban environment—an environment that we do see portrayed in the dark city of *Blade Runner*'s Los Angeles.[10] We see this from the top down, with wide-angle shots of the entire cityscape; we see it from above while the camera moves through the open space above the city, following the hovercars, and through the point of view shots where Deckard is looking out the window of the hovercar; but we also see bottom-up shots of this city, from the ground looking up, as when Pris walks toward the Bradbury building where Sebastian lives, and we see, through a narrow space between buildings, the larger, cybernetic-looking skyscrapers of the city in the background.

Through all of these intersecting elements—the combined pastiche of noir and sci-fi, the thematic contradiction between morality and immorality, the influence of cybernetics and cyberspace, and comic book pulp fiction—*Blade Runner* models a postmodern aesthetic, but it does so, in a way that still helps to historicize the postmodern. Thinking of the film's play with genre allegorically, it is possible to recognize the historical in a style that is supposed to signal the end of history. Genre, in other words, can here function as an allegory of history. If postmodernism has to do with the end of grand narrative, then the doubly coded, ironic citation of past styles in *Blade Runner*—and its dystopian, postapocalyptic narrative and set design—help us to map, not the future, but our own presentness. Dystopian fiction, after all, has never been about the future, but about our own present, and the bleak world of *Blade Runner* is one that depicts very well Jameson's famous statement that it is easier for us now to imagine the end of the world than the end of capitalism—something of which is also portrayed in the film's depiction of the postindustrial, cybernetic city.

The cybernetic city

The city is of particular importance because of its centrality in *modern* urbanism, and because of its depiction in modern cinema. The city, as represented in modern films of the silent period, such as Fritz Lang's *Metropolis* (1926), avant-garde films, like Dziga Vertov's *Man with a Movie Camera* (1929) and Walter Ruttman's *Berlin: Symphony of a Metropolis* (1927), and even in Charlie Chaplin's *Modern Times* (1936), depict one that is overrun by alienation and alienating technology, producing what Walter Benjamin referred to as a shock effect of the sensory. For the sociologist Georg Simmel, the overstimulation of the sensory brought forth by new urban technologies fashioned artificial conditions of living that created feelings of anomie accompanied by a blasé attitude that added to existing feelings of alienation.[11] In the later modern cinema of the early sound period, as with much of modernism, New York was the site of focus, particularly in the noir cinema of the 1940s and 1950s, but also in later modern films and emerging neo-noir films, like Martin Scorsese's *Taxi Driver* (1976). One thing that distinguishes postmodern films from modern films that place an emphasis on the city, like *Blade Runner*, is the change from the east coast metropolis of New York City, to the west coast emerging metropolises of cities like Los Angeles. *Pulp Fiction* is based in Los Angeles, as are other postmodern films, like Kathryn Bigelow's *Strange Days* (1995), *Memento*, and David Lynch's *Mulholland Drive* (2001), to name only a few. Just as cities like Las Vegas are postmodern for the way they draw upon a new kind of aesthetic populism born of the eclectic array of urbanism and theme park amusement, the west coast cities in postmodern films combine the architectural utopianism of the postmodern hyperspaces of buildings like the Westin Bonaventure Hotel, and pay homage to the vernacular of the anyplace of middle America. Though, they are also characterized by their ambiguous relationship to their setting. Luc Besson's *The Fifth Element* (1997) exemplifies this in film, for instance, as it takes place in New York City, but it combines a bright and sunny California-like setting with the techno-future of *Blade Runner*-style flying cars, and the revived amusement park–like kitschy tackiness of 1990s Times Square.

Blade Runner is exemplary of the kinds of postmodern portrayals of the city that we find in later cyberpunk and neo-noir films, like *Strange Days*, *Johnny Mnemonic*, and *The Matrix*. The first image that we see in *Blade Runner* is of a dark cityscape at night, shot from above, with bright yellow dots of light emanating from the buildings below. We are told at the end of the opening titles that the film takes place in Los Angeles, but the opening shot recalls, in some ways, a darker depiction of Phoenix, Arizona, in the first shot in Alfred Hitchcock's *Psycho* (1960). But unlike the opening of *Psycho*, it is evident that the Los Angeles of *Blade Runner* is a "postindustrial" city. The large flames that spring up from the buildings provide a reference to industrialism, but the mix of dark and light spots spread across the screen flatten out the image of the city to create the "look" of the "cybernetic." The city looks almost like a large computer chip. The representation, here the depiction of the city, it seems, is modeled on the computer. Depth is added as a hover car appears from the distance and approaches the foreground. Though we are told before the opening shot that this is the year 2019, the projection of the hover car deepens the depiction of the postindustrial, cybernetic city. The shot of the city cuts to an image of a blue eyeball, reflecting the sparkling lights of the city. The overlap between the eye and the image of the cybernetic city seems to mesh the human with the robotic, a theme that dominates this film. The film then cuts back to the image of the city, but from a lower perspective, allowing us to see tall columns, beyond which lie the pyramidal Tyrell buildings, themselves looking like computers inverted from the inside out. This image of the city recalls the Borg cube from *Star Trek: The Next Generation* (1987–1994), itself a mix of industrial and postindustrial/cybernetic imagery and aesthetics. It also recalls the image of the city portrayed in *Metropolis* (1926). The glossy image of the city is enhanced by the addition of large digital screens and neon signs, which we see as we follow Deckard and Gaff in the hover car that traverses the city. The large digital billboards make Los Angeles look more like Times Square in New York City, or Shibuya in Tokyo.

This glossy surface image of the dark city in *Blade Runner* contrasts with the later, street level image in the film. The street level is an underworld, full of decay, crowds, and crowdedness; it is a rather dirty depiction of a multicultural ghetto. We see "punks" and scavengers populating the streets. In the city center, the culture appears to be predominantly Asian and orientalised. Images of Chinese dragons appear on the sides of buildings, and the letters of Japanese katakana adorn the sides of buildings, stores, and restaurants/saloons. The film makes it appear as though the third world has come to Los Angeles.[12]

The look of the cyberpunk city figures the postmodern in another way as well. What Jameson refers to as "postmodern hyperspace," discussing John Portman's Bonaventure Hotel, is somewhat apt to describe the image of the city in *Blade Runner* and in other postmodern cyberpunk films. Jameson suggests that this new hyperspace transcends the individual's ability to locate herself perceptually in her immediate surroundings, or to map her position in the world.[13] His claim, here, derives in part from the recognition that with the postmodern incredulity toward metanarratives, where time and history seem to shrug in importance to space, the subject finds difficulty in grasping her own position vis-à-vis herself *and* her relationships with others. The Bonaventure figures postmodernism both concretely and metaphorically. Concretely, it is constructed as a kind of miniature city within a city, where the entrances and exits make it difficult to discern the boundaries between inside and out. Metaphorically, then, the Bonaventure identifies the difficulty of the subject to gain access to her own surroundings and environment, for which she must figuratively grow new organs in order to acclimatize. This space—a postmodern hyperspace—serves to aestheticize, in a way, the new communicational networks of decentered multinational capitalism, on the one hand, and on the other, the abstract inner space of the computer.

Tron, more so than *Blade Runner*, literalizes the aestheticizing of the inner workings of the computer and the digital, with characters themselves personifying computer programs. The cyberspace of Gibson's *Neuromancer* adds another layer to our imaginings of network and digital interaction. But *Blade Runner*'s vision of the city also seems to represent the figurative shift from the portrayal of modern industrial technologies to the "information society." Cyberpunk as a genre helped to construct and map the newly confusing inner workings of digital data circulation,[14] and in *Blade Runner* this is effected by the representation of the city *as* network. Network is also an apt metaphor for the representation of space itself in the film.

World creation

A key feature of postmodernism is its "spatialization" of time. Postmodernism, as we have seen, is less interested with questions of time and history, and puts greater emphasis on the production of space. In part, this has to do with the postmodern "incredulity toward metanarratives." But where it *is* interested in time and history, postmodernism is careful to avoid goal-oriented and teleological conceptions of time, and logics of causation or determination. In this sense, postmodernism has been more interested in surface levels rather than with "depth models." Time and space are thematized throughout *Blade Runner*. Attention to the surficial is evident in the film, both thematically and in terms of its visual presentation.

As I've already mentioned above, much of the aesthetic of *Blade Runner* is one of a retrofitted future. The future Los Angeles is recognizable because it merely tacks on new and updated technology to our familiar present. Unlike previous styles in sci-fi cinema, which often present cleaner and more sterile environments—environments that typically depict a cold, unhuman dystopia—*Blade Runner*'s future world merely updates and adds to the existing environment of postindustrial consumer society and spectacle. Known and recognizable brand logos—such as those for Coca-Cola, Atari, and Pan Am—are everywhere in this world, as are remnants of contemporary buildings and monuments in Los Angeles, such as the Bradbury building, which was built in 1894 and declared a National Historical Monument in 1977. In the film, a gutted Bradbury still exists and is the home of J. F. Sebastian. This type of augmentation of the city, mixing the old with the new, reflects a postmodern sense of space and architecture. Unlike modern architecture, which was keen to design and plan entire city spaces uniformly, focusing on the functionality of buildings, with straight edges and without frills or adornment, postmodern space is much more eclectic. Instead of focusing on functionality and planning, on the one hand postmodern buildings are designed to exhibit human liveability and form over function, and on the other hand, postmodernism seeks to bring back decoration and ornamentation into the design of buildings. Because of this, the postmodern city sees a mix of old and new in two different ways: first, in the way that older buildings exist alongside newer buildings, and second, in the way that new buildings are doubly-coded—as Charles Jencks describes—so that they create a populist sensibility or sentimentality, along with styles that reflect tradition and classicism. The Bradbury, then, is a sign of the kind of double-coding that Jencks speaks of: it is a sign of the past and of tradition. But its decay in the film displays it as a sign of the old, existing alongside the spectacle of neon and the new. The mapping of the Bradbury in its relation to the Tyrell building, for instance, shows how the film puts on display the dialectic of the old and the new in a moment of standstill—that is, where the new does not replace the old, as in the modern Faustian style of constantly evaporating the old in the fashioning of the new. The two exist in parallel so as to avoid the negation of the one by the other. *Blade Runner*'s aesthetic is then one of layering the new next to, rather than on top of, the old. The layers are visually present, seen through the density of the representation in the film.

Blade Runner's attention to space, and the layered density of its representation of the dystopian future, is featured by its capacity to build a "world." Again, like *Star Wars*, *Blade Runner* goes further than most previous sci-fi films in the way that it pays special attention to the detail of the realism of the world that it depicts. Apart from establishing the character and look of the city, the film is also populated with believable personalities and characters. *Blade Runner* doesn't just provide a representation of a single alien Other, typified to look different from the human characters. For one thing, the replicants look human and in this sense are indistinguishable as Others at the level of appearance. The culture of the city is also diverse, a combination of an Asiatic/Near Eastern cultural mosaic, where Chinatown meets the orientalism of a film like *Raiders of the Lost Ark* (1980). There is a distinction between the slum of the city, down below, and the spaces of the elite higher up in the pyramidal high rises of the Tyrell corporation and Tyrell's own penthouse apartment.[15] The advertisements and the discussion of the Off-World colonies show that the world of *Blade Runner* is not limited to planet Earth. These advertisements depict a dualism between center and periphery, where the advertisements for the colonies seem to mimic the suburban sprawl of the 1950s and 1960s: as heard from the advertisement, "A new life awaits you in the off world colonies!" Just as *Star Wars* creates a world of diverse characters, with distinct personalities—the droids, R2D2 and C3P0, and secondary alien characters like the gangster Jaba the Hutt, the bounty hunter Boba Fett, the rebel fleet commander Admiral Ackbar, and the loveable impish Jedi master Yoda—*Blade Runner* represents a rich level of detail in both the background of the story and in its use of visual space.

Spatially, the film also models the postmodern network of multinational capitalism, and the way that postindustrial production is often the product of a vast global array of contractual and subcontractual relationships between corporations and manufacturers. It is noted throughout the film that the Tyrell Corporation does not produce the replicants all by itself. In fact, the film addresses how the corporation subcontracts out, to different producers and manufacturers, the construction of the different parts of the replicants that are later assembled. Chew, for instance, makes only the eyes of the replicants; Sebastian works on the mind or brain of the replicants. In other examples, smaller manufacturers like Abdul Ben-Hassan, the maker of Zhora's electronic snake, shows just how vast the network of replicant manufacturing truly is in the world of *Blade Runner*. This network of production narrativizes the global/spatialized present of the postmodern. Added to this is still the consumer spectacle space of the brand logos that adorn the city, still another indication of the "end of history" sensibility of the film, where often dystopia serves to emphasize that it is no longer possible to imagine coherent alternatives to late, consumer capitalism.

Techno-space, simulation, and the hyperreal

The film deals with space in other interesting ways too, not least of which is the scene where Deckard uses the Esper machine to conduct part of his investigation into the whereabouts of the escaped replicants. Deckard uses the machine to enhance and navigate through one of the still photographs found in Leon's apartment. Inserting the photograph into the machine, the image is then displayed on a computer-TV monitor, overlaid with a grid. Deckard uses the grid to call out the coordinates of a particular area of the image that he wishes to investigate. He calls out commands, such as: "Enhance 2–24 to 176," a command that closes in on and enlarges the specific area of the photograph that he wishes to examine.[16] As the machine closes in on this area of the photograph, it continues to make sounds simulating the shutter of an analog camera. Deckard uses other commands, typical of film direction: "Pull out, track right." He examines the image as would a regular detective investigate and search for clues in a room at the "scene of the crime." Through his interrogation of the image, Deckard locates Zhora next to an object that reminds him of the small piece of simulated animal skin he found earlier when looking around Leon's apartment. His investigation of the image therefore leads Deckard forward in his search for the replicants.

The scene with the Esper machine intriguingly figures the postmodern theme of flatness and the surficial, and the waning of depth. Deckard uses the machine to navigate and dig beneath the surface of the image. Instead of the three-dimensional space of the room itself, and the "scene of the crime," so to speak, the two-dimensional surface of the image provides Deckard with the very information that he seeks. He *un*covers what is directly present on the surface of the photograph. The photograph as analyzed by the Esper machine thus becomes a hyperreal space. It is almost a digital version of the type of investigation that we see in films like Michelangelo Antonioni's *Blow-Up* (1961), in which a photographer accidentally snaps a shot showing evidence of a murder taking place—he enlarges the photograph (he creates a "blow-up" of the picture) to investigate the scene; or Brian De Palma's *Blow Out* (1981), based on Antonioni's film, which detects evidence of a murder taking place on an audio recording. The Esper machine is then a digital postmodern counterpart to the analog modern investigations taking place in these films. The Esper machine also prefigures the examination of digital space in virtual reality.

Deckard is able to explore the photograph in this way because it becomes a space of virtual reality. It is a virtual reality unlike that depicted in *The Matrix*, *The Lawnmower Man* (Brett Leonard, 1992), or *The Thirteenth Floor* (Josef Rusnak, 1999). In *The Matrix* and *The Thirteenth Floor*, for instance, virtual reality substitutes for the reality of the protagonist. The "reality" in these films is pure simulation, putting into question the ontological status of reality as such. Is our reality real or is it mere illusion? *The Lawnmower Man* narrativizes virtual reality, which is presented more like a video game that the characters can play. It is not meant to substitute for "real" reality, but the film deals with the question of how the mind can handle existing in two different types of reality—one real, and the other simulated. In *Blade Runner*, VR is not yet part of the popular tech lingo in cyber culture. But the search through the photograph using the

Esper machine creates, in a way, an alternate simulated reality within the surface of the image, which allows Deckard to navigate its terrain digitally. The surface space of the photograph is penetrated. It is no longer simply a still image. The Esper machine allows Deckard to move around in this still environment: he can look more closely, look "around" walls. It is in this way transformed into a digital hyperspace. The Esper machine allows Deckard to "enter" the image in a way that was not possible through the naked eye.

Technologies of simulation and enhancement operate in other ways too in the film. Just as the Esper machine supplements the detective capabilities of the human eye technologically, the Voight-Kampff test amplifies through a technological device as well the ability of the eye to discover the differences between humans and replicants. The screen of the Voight-Kampff test displays and enlarges the eye of the test subject. Again, eyes return as part of the imagery of the film. There is the "floating" eye at the beginning of the film that looks out upon the cityscape—the eye that is never subjectivized, shown to belong to any of the characters. Eyes are also put on display in the scene in Chew's eye manufacturing lab, where he figures out that Roy is a replicant by looking into his eyes; clearly Chew would not need to use a Voight-Kampff test to discern between humans and replicants. Tyrell's eyes are also plucked out by Roy in the end. Eyes, then, seem to be for the film a marker of the bodily difference between replicants and humans. But it is only because of the technological "eye," the use of machinery like the Voight-Kampff test, and the Esper machine that humans are able to detect the replicants. Humans, too, require the enhancement of technology in order to "see." We are, as Donna Haraway put it, all "cyborgs," in the end.

This is a theme that comes across in several films directed by David Cronenberg, who has given much attention to the relationship between the human body, technology, and media/mediation. Two films in particular are worth noting: *Videodrome* (1983) and *eXistenZ* (1998). The former is reflective of the McLuhanesque media theory, of the notion that media extend the human sensory—it is, to cite the subtitle of his most famous book, an "extension of man." In *Videodrome*, the hero becomes physically attached to media technology, as his body meshes with the media that he uses: the television, a primitive variation on VR technology, a video cassette, even a gun molds into his hand. *eXistenZ* can be thought of as an unofficial sequel to *Videodrome*, where similar themes arise, tied to the bind between the corporeal and the technological. In the film, the characters play in a VR environment that they "port" into through an input in their back, connected to their spine, called a "bioport." The characters play around in different VR environments, trying to solve a mystery, engaging in battle. There are conspiracy theories abounding, but they are never certain whether or not they are still in the game. The game console is made out of organic material, and at one point when the console breaks down from a virus, it is repaired in a scene that looks more like cardiac surgery than the workshop of a machinist. In a few key moments in the film, a gun made of bones and teeth is used to attack and kill, a reflection, perhaps, of how technology doesn't always have to appear "technological," or perhaps even a commentary on the technological side of human identity. In the same way, the replicants—artificial life forms/androids—are made of organic material and look human, not only on the outside, but we can expect—based on the scene in Chew's lab and the discussion about the manufacturing of the NEXUS's eyes—on the inside as well. But if they are organic and not mechanical beings, what then distinguishes them from humans?

Schizoid androids and Oedipal subjects

If the film's play with genre, its use of pastiche, its mise-en-scène, set design, and world creation all work to spatialize time and history, then it is by troubling conceptions of humanity and identity that the film brings in and questions modern conceptions of subjectivity. However, as we will see, the way subjectivity is questioned in *Blade Runner* still allows us to historicize postmodernism in interesting ways. One way that the film bridges the modern and the postmodern—or at least registers a historical moment of transition with the broader culture of late capitalism—is seen in the dialectical tension between the "schizoid android" and the attempt to Oedipalize the replicants.

N. Katharine Hayles describes the "schizoid android" as a type of character that reappears in Dick's novels.[17] This character, she says, is often female, emotionally distant, and unable to feel empathy. The schizoid android usually brings together the qualities of being both literally a machine—she is often a robot/android, like the replicants in *Blade Runner*—and acts machine-like: computational, emotionally shut off, and logical. Pris Stratton and Rachael Rosen in *Do Androids Dream of Electric Sheep?* are paradigmatic examples, but another popular example might be commander Data from *Star Trek: The Next Generation*. He demonstrates perfectly the qualities of being literally a machine—much more so than the replicants. Throughout the series, we often see images of the cybernetic wires and flashing lights operating beneath his skin, whereas the replicants are portrayed as much more organic—and his manner of thinking and speaking are rather machine-like: he is cold, incapable of emotion, and logical, though he does demonstrate empathy toward others on numerous occasions.

Jameson, and Deleuze and Guattari, as we have seen, all posit the schizo as typical of postmodern subjectivity. For Deleuze and Guattari, it is precisely the market mechanisms of capitalism that work toward unhinging fixed meanings and narratives that (in)form the basis of modern, liberal, bourgeois subjectivity. Jameson, similarly, notes that the schizo serves as a good aesthetic model for understanding the postmodern breakdown of both history and subjectivity. We saw in Chapter One that Jameson uses the Lacanian formula—the "breakdown of the signifying chain"—to describe the postmodern loss of "historicity" as well as the conception of the "death of the subject." *Blade Runner* applies this theme to the material and visual signifier of the photograph, which signifies the over-lapping losses of history *and* subjectivity. Jameson notes that the loss of the referent, the loss of the signifier—the word, object, image that holds meaning together—makes it difficult for the subject to locate herself in time and space, and creates difficulty in producing (new) meaning(s). In the spatial form of language, this loss means that we are unable to link together or think the past, present, and future within the single sentence. In terms of the psychic life of the individual, this means similarly that we experience a loss of sense in the distinctions between past, present, and future. As Jameson explains, this means that the schizo experiences the world in terms of unrelated material signifiers of meaning, or in terms of unrelated moments of present time—a "perpetual present."[18]

We might also consider reading the breakdown of the signifying chain at a formal level in the film—that is, if we compare the original US Theatrical Release with the Director's Cut and the Final Cut. With the addition of the unicorn scene, and the loss of the original ending, with Deckard and Rachael driving up north, it is almost as if we witness the entry of a repressed desire into the symbolic space of the film, marked by the foreclosure of the scene of the happy couple in the end. The editing of the film, in this way, mirrors the postmodern conceptualization of history and subjectivity. Compare this, for instance, with a three-and-a-half second shot of a light tower at night from Michael Curtiz's *Casablanca* (1942), which separates a scene of Rick and Ilsa embracing from one where they are simply engaged in conversation. The shot of the light tower is added in order to disavow the possibility that Rick and Ilsa have had sex. The added shot in between these two scenes allows the film formally to repress this content.[19] Similarly, the tacked-on ending to the original US Theatrical Release of *Blade Runner* shows the unification of the happy couple; but the Director's Cut forecloses this scene, and adds in the extra (previously "repressed") content of the unicorn dream sequence, thus rendering the repressed fantasy in the visible space of the film. The repressed content and its implied meaning—that Deckard is a replicant—now forms part of the diegetic space of the film. The formerly repressed content is now made visible to the gaze of the spectator. The original US Theatrical Release in this way sides with a subject formation that is much closer to the neurotic of modernism, whereas the rendering of the fantasy in the space of the film shows the Director's Cut to be much more congruent with the portrayal of the characters in the rest of the film. Nevertheless, this fact is only recognizable in the relationship between the two versions of the film, and in this way, *Blade Runner* formally attends to the split between schizo and neurotic. I'd like to make this a bit more apparent by referring to another example.

The schizo figures prominently in other postmodern films, but especially in David Fincher's *Fight Club* (1999). The film, based on the novel by Chuck Palahniuk, tells the story of an unnamed protagonist (Edward Norton), who is also the film's narrator. The narrator works as an actuary for a major car company, assessing defects in cars sold on the market, and helps to make decisions about the worthiness of a recall. The film throughout is tied thematically to late 1990s anticonsumerist activism of the variety that culminated in the publications of Kalle Lasn's *Culture Jam* (1999), Naomi Klein's *No Logo* (2000), and the WTO protest in Seattle in 1999. In the film, the narrator first introduces himself by speaking of how he identifies with commodities and commodification in the form of the consumerism of the Ikea catalogue—describing the items in his apartment, he sounds like the catalogue itself, as catalogue descriptions, accompanying each item, are displayed on the screen. The film, though, begins with the narrator visiting a series of support groups in churches and community centers for people suffering from a series of traumas. The first group he visits is one for men with testicular cancer, and one of the first shots of the film shows the narrator being embraced tightly by an overweight man (played by the singer Meatloaf) who has grown breasts from a loss of testosterone, a sign of his literal castration. We learn that the narrator suffers from insomnia, and visits these groups as part of his own coping mechanism. He later meets Tyler Durden (Brad Pitt), who we discover is the narrator's alter ego—the narrator, in fact, has a dual personality disorder and Tyler is actually his alternate personality.

The narrator and Tyler form the fight club, which becomes both a support group for men—helping them to reclaim an aspect of their typical machismo and bravado, lost according to the film because of an overabundance of "feminizing" consumerism—and later, the group transforms into an activist/"terrorist" group, called Project Mayhem. As a sign of the film's anticonsumerist/Adbusters-like critique, at one point in the film, the narrator and Tyler see a Calvin Klein underwear advertisement on the bus, showing a hairless, muscular "pretty boy." Pointing to the ad, the narrator says: "Is that what a real man is supposed to look like?" Though the film appears critical of capitalism and consumerism (the final "act" of the fight club at the end of the film is blowing up the head offices of the major credit card companies), this is mixed with a rather chauvinistic portrayal of masculinity, the loss of which the film seems to identify with post-Fordist consumerism.[20] With the fight club, the characters in the film seem to be literally attempting to beat both consumerism and its feminizing qualities out of themselves. They are, in a sense, attempting to regain the lost phallic signifier—the paternal authority—of late, Fordist, modernism.

The narrator's insomnia, and dislocation of himself between waking and sleeping time, his split between himself and Tyler (is he really Tyler? Is Tyler really him?) is a sign of his lack of fixed identity, typical of the postmodern subject. In the film, this dislocation is tied to the background of consumer/post-Fordist capitalism. The film is also structured to mirror the narrator's/Tyler's loss of temporal depth, and is presented almost out of joint—it is nonlinear. The narration re-marks the linearity of the narrative. Narration works, in a way, to fix the protagonist in time and space. It is a way of grounding and mapping himself, not unlike the talking cure in psychoanalysis. Similarly, in *Blade Runner*, implanted memories and the use of photographs help to mark and ground the temporality and history of its characters.

Because of their loss, or lack of memory, but also because they lack the security afforded by "personhood," the replicants, including and especially Rachael, represent the schizo subject, but in a different way. Rachael, more so than the other replicants, represents the process of transition from a typical neurotic to a schizo subject because we witness her experience of the loss of the referent that ties together her subjective experience. The photograph and her memories are discredited. All of who she was, her ability to locate herself in time and space, is obliterated, and she is forced into the experience of a perpetual present. Deckard, too, in the Director's Cut and after, is schizoid in this way. When he finds Gaff's origami unicorn, the *presence* of this material signifier—which is added, it is a surplus, rather than a loss or lack—in a way unhinges his own unified, individual sense of self. His memory/daydream of the unicorn becomes public, it is no longer private, and in this way he loses the individuality and uniqueness of modern bourgeois subjectivity. This is never discussed at the diegetic level of the film, but through the visual combination of the unicorn dream sequence and the shot of the origami figure left by Gaff, the film visually and implicitly questions Deckard's status as human.

Both Leon and Roy, though, show how this experience of schizo subjectivity—of a perpetual present—is felt by the escaped replicants. As he is about to kill Deckard, before Rachael saves him, Leon says: "Painful to live in fear, isn't it?" Later, when Deckard is hanging from the rooftop, just before saving him Roy says: "Quite an experience to live in fear, isn't it? That's what it is to be a slave." Not only are the replicants typical schizo subjects for the fact of being artificial life forms, and for lacking a biography, they live in pure and unrelated moments in time for the fact of being constantly on the run, never secure or free to think of the long term; they exist in a perpetual present.

Intriguingly, though, the film borders the modern and the postmodern, as the replicants are to a degree Oedipalized. The "mommy-daddy-me" relationship, as Deleuze and Guattari put it, returns at several key moments throughout the film. Both time and personal history in the film are Oedipal, with origins of desire tied to the mother/maternal relationship, and questions of destiny tied to the father/paternal. The question that first plagues Leon at the beginning of the film is one about his mother, one that he obviously never had. Rachael's implanted memories are about her mother. Meanwhile, Tyrell is treated as a paternal figure. He is the male/masculine creator of the replicants, with dominating authority—over the replicants, and it would appear throughout the world of *Blade Runner*. He is the postindustrial king/master, sitting atop the overarching pyramidal structures that overlook the city. It is interesting that in the original US Theatrical Release, when Roy confronts Tyrell near the end of the film, just prior to plucking out his eyes with his thumbs and killing him, he demands of Tyrell: "I want more life, fucker!" In the Final Cut, this scene is changed in two ways: first, a shot edited from the original US Theatrical Release but included in the International Theatrical Release, showing the violence of Tyrell's face as Roy plucks out his eyes—a much bloodier, gorier scene—is included; second, the line "I want more life, fucker," has been changed to "I want more life, father." Clearly, with Tyrell identified as the paternal figure here, the film posits the Oedipalization of the replicants in another way, as the scene references *Oedipus Rex*, who plucked out his own eyes. Oedipalization and the Oedipal structure serves to historicize the replicants. It gives them a history by giving them an origin, even if it is one that is symbolically structured as "mommy-daddy-me."

Though it does this, it still calls into question—similar to postmodern critical theory—such an essential aspect of modern identity. By showing that "mommy" and "daddy" serve symbolic functions, rather than biological ones in our psychic life, the film suggests that we should read human subjectivity through the prism of lack in the replicants. *Blade Runner* suggests that there is nothing essential to subjectivity, and therefore that the subject—the bourgeois, liberal subject of modernity—does not exist (the subject is "dead"), and is more an ideological manifestation of existing relations of power. The replicants, then, more so than the human characters in the film (including Deckard in the original US Theatrical Release and later) represent the basic elements of subjectivity.

History and retroactivity

Much attention is paid in *Blade Runner* to the relationship between photographs and other documentary evidence of history and time, memory, and identity. In fact, the film reminds us that history comes to us primarily in symbolic or representational form. That is, we only ever come to know history through documentary evidence, like historical documents, books, paintings and photographs, films, audio recordings, and the like. These various media *represent* history, presenting it through a particular formal model, matrix, and structure. But what happens when we "lose" the document itself? What happens, in other words, when the authenticity of the document, the reference to real history, is delegitimized or discredited? What happens to our sense of history and our relationship to it—that is, what happens to our sense of self and our identity, formed through our own personal historical memories, as well as our identification with a set of cultural memories—when the reference is lost? This is thematized in Christopher Nolan's *Memento*, where the hero, Leonard, loses all of his short-term memory, and instead uses polaroid photographs to document his recent encounters. Leonard is trying to track down his wife's murderers, but since he narrativizes his investigation through his polaroids, we see throughout the film how easily his own personal narrative becomes disjointed and difficult to document. In the end, we see how he even fools himself into killing the wrong man, his friend Teddy. As Mark Fisher puts it, "[in] conditions where realities and identities are upgraded like software, it is not surprising that memory disorders should have become the focus of cultural anxiety."[21] In *Blade Runner*, Rachael and the other replicants, including Deckard after the Director's Cut, are forced to deal with these questions of how to conceptualize the self and one's own personal history through the documentary evidence of photographs.

When Rachael tracks down Deckard to prove to him that she is not a replicant but a human, her evidence is a photograph of her with her mother. Though, as Deckard tells her, she is not really the little girl in the photograph. It is, rather, a photo of Tyrell's niece. Deckard continues, asking her if she remembers the time when she was six years old, when she and her brother "snuck into an empty building through a basement window—you were going to play doctor. He showed you his, and when it got to be your turn you chickened and ran. Remember that?" He goes on, "You remember the spider that lived in a bush outside your window? Orange body, green legs; watched her build a web all summer. Then one day there's a big egg in it; the egg hatched and ..." Rachael interrupts: "The egg hatched, and a hundred baby spiders came out ... and they ate her." Deckard asks her in order to double check his own information: Did she ever tell anybody about these memories? Her mother? Tyrell? She says no. The fact that *he* knows these very personal memories—memories that seem to connect to Rachael's personal history, her sense of identity—delegitimizes her personal selfhood. What she believed were private memories—memories that only she knew—become in that moment public. Their publicity challenges their authenticity, and thus the authenticity of her humanity. Deckard tells her that her memories are implanted—they aren't *her* memories; they belong to someone else.

Earlier, Tyrell tells Deckard that the reason for implanting memories in the new generation of the NEXUS replicants is to help structure their sense of affect. As Bryant tells him in his briefing about the escaped replicants, and as Tyrell later confirms, detection of emotion was noticed in the NEXUS 6. Tyrell explains that without any biographical context for how to deal with their emotions, the replicants might act erratically. Fearing that they'd be unable to deal with the onset of emotion, having no personal experience with emotions—most likely because they are "born" as adults, *without* a childhood—the implantation of memories was a necessary fail safe method, used not to control the replicants, but to help them to structure their relationship to their emotional responses. It is precisely her ability to structure her relationship to her emotions that allows Rachael to get so far into the Voight-Kampff test without being detected as a replicant until the very end of the test. By making the link between memories and their referentiality in documents like photographs, *Blade Runner* calls into question the depth models, and the language of authenticity and autonomy upon which modern liberal/bourgeois conceptions of subjectivity depend: this is the "real me;" below the surface level, there is an essential identity that belongs to me. If memories can be implanted—if emotions can be replicated in androids and artificial intelligence—what then is truly "human" about humans? Is there an *essence* to our humanity? If history, similarly—documented history—can be fabricated, if the reference to real history is lost, removed, what then *is* history, if it is not an accounting of real events? As Michel Foucault explains in his essay "Nietzsche, Genealogy, History,"[22] the search for historical origins (essence) ultimately fails for the very reasons proposed in *Blade Runner*. Historical documents, references to "real" history, are themselves often still fallacious. History, as the search for origins—for "essence"—is therefore either based upon a false premise, or else it is overladen with ideology.

Psychoanalysis offers an alternative explanation of the film's invocation of historical memory. Kaja Silverman notes that the film renders quite descriptively, in fact, the process discovered by Freud, called "retroactivity," where the present "rewrites" or reorganizes—restages, ultimately—in a manner of speaking, memories of the past. Older memories may be retroactively restaged because of some trigger in the present, marking the past memory anew with trauma.

What Freud called "screen memories," similarly, stand in for repressed fantasies and other memories that are prevented from becoming conscious. These screen memories are largely fabrications. Conceived in this way, Silverman highlights the fact that our memories are in fact no more real than Rachael's.[23] Rachael is deemed nonhuman or inhuman because her memories are false. However, according to Silverman's argument, all of our memories are to some degree false: our past is always being rewritten, in a manner of speaking, from the perspective of the present. We can also consider how retroactivity operates on history and historical evidence.

History, we might say, from the perspective of retroactivity, is always a history of the present. As Foucault puts it, "History is that which transforms documents into monuments." Or, put differently, history is "one way in which a society recognizes and develops mass documentation with which it is inextricably linked."[24] The present moment retroactively re-cites and rearranges the past seen through the representation found in the form of the documentary evidence. This postmodern thesis about history enables us, as well, to rethink the form of the pastiche found in the film's generic style. What we get in the combination of noir and sci-fi is *not* the historical past. It is, rather, a retroactive treatment of the historical memory of the representation of these generic styles. The styles themselves are not cited; it is rather stereotypical representations of these styles that are recoded into the form of the film and its presentation. In a way, the focus on the photographs in the film are demonstrative of its own self-reflexivity—its own self-consciousness—as to the quality of its form: by dislodging the characters from the historical past found in the photographs as evidence, the film teaches us that the historical past is part of an ideological construction, and one that originates in the present rather than the past. The present, so to speak, retroactively ties together its own prior historical "determinants."

The Director's Cut delves deeper into this thesis when it puts into question the status of Deckard's humanity. About midway through the film, Deckard is seen leaning his elbow on his piano, resting his head on his fist, playing a few keys. On top of the piano are photographs, portraits, of what are presumably his ancestors. Who are the people in these portraits? We don't know. They remain ambiguous. Later on, looking at the photographs, Rachael pulls down her hair, changing it somewhat to reflect a hairstyle seen in one of Deckard's photos. The style of the photographs is also not what we would expect in this depiction of a futuristic society. They are black-and-white daguerreotypes, mostly. A reference to a technology of visual representation dating back to the mid-nineteenth century. The scene where Deckard lays his head down on the piano appears just prior to his use of the Esper machine to investigate Leon's photograph, and just after the scene where he informs Rachael about the falsehood of the picture she uses to document her own past. Immediately after he tells her this undoubtedly traumatic information, she drops the photo on the ground and leaves. Deckard goes to pick up the photo, and then turns to the pile of photographs that he found at Leon's apartment, selecting the one that he later chooses to investigate. There is a close-up on the photograph of Rachael/Tyrell's niece and her mother, followed by a close up of Leon's photographs. They are signifiers, references, to real history. Objects that signify the fact that this history, the events, have occurred. But have they really?

In the original US Theatrical Release, the scene where Deckard is resting next to the piano transitions into the scene with the Esper machine. In the Director's Cut, however, a new shot is "implanted." The scene where Deckard is resting near the piano now includes cuts to a scene of a unicorn running through the forest. The scene passes back and forth between Deckard and the unicorn. Deckard's eyes are open, so we know that he is not dreaming. The Final Cut includes longer takes of the unicorn, as well as additional angles of Deckard at the piano, making the sequence a bit longer than it appears in the Director's Cut. Deckard then takes Leon's photo and goes to the Esper machine. Retroactivity is a term that describes how this new "implanted" scene changes (or for some, affirms) the meaning of the film's conclusion, when he leaves his apartment with Rachael and finds the origami unicorn left by Gaff. In all versions of the film, we then hear Gaff's lines, recalled by Deckard, saying: "It's too bad she won't live. But then again, who does?" In the original ending, in the original US Theatrical Release, this scene is followed by the happy ending where Deckard and Rachael escape into the natural setting north of the city, and is accompanied by Deckard's voiceover narration, saying, "Gaff had been there, and let her [Rachael] live. Four years, he figured. He was wrong. Tyrell told me that Rachael was special: no termination date. I didn't know how long we had together, who does?" The narration, here, is meant to close the gap left open by the origami unicorn Deckard finds outside his apartment door. In the Director's Cut, the final scene is removed, as is the voiceover narration, and with the addition of the implanted unicorn scene midway through the film, we are now presented with the idea that Deckard, too, is a replicant. This is alluded to in the original US Theatrical Release, when Rachael asks Deckard: "You know that Voight-Kampff test of yours? Did you ever take that test yourself?" Deckard's status as a replicant is then solidified by the new ending of the Director's Cut. If Deckard is not a replicant, then how did Gaff know about the unicorn? How does Deckard know about Rachael's memory of the spider?

Race, class, and replicants

If Deckard is a replicant, is Roy then a person? The obvious answer is surely no—they are *both* replicants. However, throughout the course of the film, Deckard *is* treated like a person, while Roy is not. Rachael, like Deckard, is initially treated as a person. That is, we, the audience, see her as a person until she fails the Voight-Kampff test. But why should some be put in the position of human/person, and others in the position of replicant? Again, the obvious answer is that the replicants are simulations; they are artificial life forms. We have already seen, though, that the film encourages us to search for alternative definitions of humanity since, if we define humanness according to ability to feel emotions, or by our identification with our memories, then that definition slips away when we realize that, on the one hand, emotions can be the product of a surface effect, reacting to our memories, and on the other hand, our memories too are not necessarily based in actual factual or real history. So this definition will not do. What, then, about the bodies of the replicants? Can this be the basis of distinguishing the difference between humans and replicants? Sebastien, upon figuring out that Roy and Pris are replicants, says: "Show me something." Roy responds, saying: "We're not computers, Sebastian. We're physical."

It is worth drawing attention to the fact that replicants are created and manufactured to be servants/slaves to humans. They are meant to serve humans on the "suburban" Off-World colonies. It is also worth pointing out that distinguishing between master and servant based on essential differences in the type of body that they possess is a form of biological determinism, racism as well as sexism. But again, the film evokes questions over the differences that allot some into positions of power and others into positions of exploitation and oppression. By questioning the essence of Rachael's, as well as Deckard's identity, *Blade Runner* troubles the opposition between master and servant, suggesting that there is no essential basis for this division. In fact, as Slavoj Žižek claims, *Blade Runner* is actually a film about the emergence of class consciousness.[25]

While the film is populated with racialized minorities, primarily through the Asian and orientalised characters in the background, it is the replicants themselves, though all white, that offer up the clearest antiessentialist arguments about race, sex, and class. In the film, the working class, the replicants—just like the droids, R2D2 and C3P0, in *Star*

Wars—are artificial life forms, and their position is determined by the bodies that they possess. Race and class intersect here, where the position of exploitation is determined by one's body. Intriguingly, because the replicants resemble humans so closely, the only way to detect the difference between bodies is to use the Voight-Kampff test. The difference is measured technologically, medically even, suggesting that this is almost a matter of eugenics, where differences are measured at the genetic level. Differences between the characters in *Gattaca*, between the working class and the elite, are similarly found at the level of the body and genetics. The latter more explicitly deals with ethical questions of eugenics, but *Blade Runner*, too, shows that marked differences between the exploited and the exploiters has come down, ultimately, to a genetic difference detectable only through "prosthetic" vision provided by the Voight-Kampff test. Like racial and sexual difference in our own culture, often used as the support for the artificial manufacturing and reproduction of inequality, the difference between humans and replicants is ideological.

This is demonstrated further in the film when Deckard is twice saved by replicants. He is saved by Rachael, first when he is being attacked by Leon, and then later by Roy, near the end of the film, when he tries to jump from one rooftop to the next. He misses and is left dangling, holding onto a crossbeam emerging from the rooftop of one of the buildings. Roy then grabs Deckard, saving his life just before he dies, himself, as his four-year lifespan has just expired. Both Rachael and Roy experience emotions. They are capable of empathy, which they both show toward Deckard. It could be argued that they are showing empathy toward Deckard because he is a replicant, and that therefore they still do not empathize with humans. However, since neither knows that Deckard is truly a replicant it would be difficult to make this claim. Instead, their empathy toward him demonstrates further just how deeply the ideology of class difference—and racism as one of its effects—makes possible the conditions of continued servitude.

Postmodern *Blade Runner*

In Chapter One, we saw that the postmodern challenge to authoritative history, and master narratives in particular, is central to postmodern critical theory, as is a shift from questions about ideology to those of representation and discourse. We saw, too, that postmodernism questions and challenges the modern fixation on the centered subject of experience, modern or liberal subjectivity and the Cartesian *Cogito*. Postmodernism, also, challenges the largely Western and phallocentric position posited by modernism as typical. As we have seen, *Blade Runner* brings to the surface some of these themes.

The play of genre, the mix of film noir and sci-fi conventions, combines pastiche and parody, and signals the film's relationship with history and historicity. These conventions are further temporalized with the added mix of the cybernetic and imagery of the digital, producing the postmodern genre of cyberpunk. Furthermore, the role of photography as a signifier of "real" history in the film demonstrates, from a postmodern perspective, just how flexible history and historical memory can be, and how easily it can be de-sutured.

Genre is also an aspect of representation that the film plays around with, but so too does the film develop this theme with its ties to technological reproducibility and simulation, and the technological enhancement of vision, with the use of the Esper and Voight-Kampff machines. Again, photography and the permeability of the image are tied in to show just how history comes to us in representational form. Even as a mediation on the film itself, Rachael, Leon, and Deckard's photographs remind viewers, particularly, in the Final Cut version of the film, that visual evidence, especially in an age of digital reproducibility, is never simply a reflection of the truth and of true history.

The film most intriguingly challenges modern liberal conceptions of subjectivity, both in terms of conscious self-awareness and in terms of the body of the subject. Here, the humanity of the replicants comes into question. What separates them from "us"? Rachael's implanted memories mark her as inhuman, but she experiences them as a sign of her real "self." Deckard's humanity too, following the Director's Cut, is put into question, with the "implantation" of the unicorn scene. The replicants are said to lack empathy, but both Rachael and Roy demonstrate concern for Deckard's life, each saving him at different points in the film.

The film "maps" the postmodern emphasis on pluralism and the critique of Eurocentrism with the very layout of the city. The cybernetic city highlights the role of the rhizomatic network model of multinational capitalism; also, in the single space of postapocalyptic Los Angeles, the film portrays a multicultural/orientalized (even with the use of "Cityspeak" in the original US Theatrical Release) depiction of postmodern hyperspace, that in some ways actualizes the imagery of post–Cold War globalization. The attention and detail paid to the layout and the "world" of the city provides a retrofitted, yet glossy depiction of the postmodern spatialization of time. Space, in *Blade Runner*, is given precedence over time, and this is particularly pronounced in the four-year lifespan of the replicants. But the surface level of space has also allowed us to read the film intertextually with other examples of postmodern cinema. What we might now consider is how the film works intertextually with other media and the context of our postmodern present more generally.

Mapping our postmodern present

One of the things that remains striking about *Blade Runner* is the way that the content of the film prefigures some of our mediated experiences in the twenty-first century, but also how the film is self-reflexive about its own status as media obeject in a way that provides insights for postmodern mediation. The film itself gives us a kind of cognitive mapping of our own historical context. But if we consider the three central types of media objects in the film—the photographs, the Esper machine, and the Voight-Kampff machine—we can see how *Blade Runner* provides for us some tools for thinking shifts in media hardware and storage technologies over the last few decades.

Not only do the various incarnations of the film—from the original US Theatrical Release, to Director's Cut, to Final Cut—provide for us a historical mapping of the different significant moments of postmodernity; these media objects provide a kind of phenomenological mapping of our own expriences with media. The photographs in the film are markers of real history. They signifiy the tie between our subjective experiences with the objectivity of the world as "real" history. But as we learn, they are mere simulacra, without any real referent. Considering the shift from the original US Theatrical Release to the Final Cut, we can see how easily digital media makes possible the elimination of the real object, of real history. What we learn, instead, is that history is the history of representations; history only comes to us in represenational form.[26] Even if we consider the transition from the film reel as a medium, to videocasette (and with it, home spectatorship), to DVD, Blu-ray, and now online streaming sites like Netflix, we see how objective history—that is, history as understood through the prism of material culture, of actual objects and artifacts—has moved away from looking at the content of data to its form. Media archaeology now teaches us that in some ways, hardware takes precedence over "software," or the content of the medium. *Blade Runner* foreshadows this, somewhat, in the way that it destabilizes Rachael's relationship to her own history via the photograph of her and her mother. The significance of the photograph is not only its content—the image of her and her mother—but also the form of the evidentiary object. Form and content overlap here, where it is the form that legitimizes the content. Because it is a photograph—because it is "objective," it is material, captured through the objective framework of the technological medium—its content is given legitimacy. However, once the content is delegitimized, when Deckard tells her that she is not the little girl in the photograph, the form also loses its authenticity.

As new forms of media storage emerge, and as media becomes lighter, its evidentiary status seems to diminish. As we move from media that we can literally hold onto (the film reel, the VHS cassette, the DVD) to streaming services, we start to see how our ties to the object, and to objective history, becomes more fluid and fungible. Also, if we take seriously the claim that live action footage is just another element of animation in digital filmmaking, then we have to consider a deeper loss in the evidentiary qualities of film and new media. New media is simply the connection of an interface to a database.[27] Changes from the original US Theatrical Release to the Final Cut, again, show us precisely where film as evidence is misleading. What we need, instead, is an objective correlate that legitimizes our own position in the world, that allows us to make our sense of self meaningful. Here, too, the film provides for us a way to think of new postmodern practices of identification.

Reflecting on the form of the "cybernetic" city, we see how the film provides a layout that spatializes the representation of postmdodern identity politics. I would propose that we can still apply the film allegorically to our present conceptualization of social media and the construction of the public profile. Social media provides another kind of spatial cognitive mapping. In the process of deligitimizing grand narratives—narratives that gave modern subjects a sense of self and position in the world—the subject's own sense of self and position become destabilized. This, in part, is contained in Deleuze and Guattari's version of schizoanalysis, where the paternal signifier is foreclosed. Social media, however, makes possible new expressions of identity in the spatial network of the internet. It provides, in other words, a form of spatial cognitive mapping, in which we can construct our identities digitally—no longer, though, just the avatar of Web 1.0; social media creates incentives and directives that prompt users to try to depict a more realistic presentation of self and selfhood.[28] In this way, too, postmodern subjectivity takes on a new mode of operation.

Though the film deals with and positions the subject between schizoid android and Oedipalization, I would argue that changes in social, cultural, and political forces of contemporary postmodernism create conditions for *perverting* the subject in the strictest Lacanian sense. For Lacan, perversion (like neurosis and psychosis) describes a specific way in which the subject relates to enjoyment. The neurotic constantly questions/doubts authority, while the psychotic experiences the loss of the existence of authority (though he still experiences the object of desire/enjoyment as something objectifiable). The pervert, however, recognizes that the object of desire exists only if it is constantly prohibited by authority, and therefore, in order to continue to enjoy, attempts to will into existence some figure of prohibiting authority. Given that, as we have seen, postmodernism commands obligatory enjoyment, the postmodern subject begins to experience the loss of authority as a *limitation* on enjoyment, and therefore, ideology, today, works by practices of willing back into existence forms of authority (after they have been decontructed by the various postmodern and post-structuralist crtiques of grand narrative and big government/authority, and even the modern authoritative voice of the West and the masculine), or what Lacan called the "big Other." Even our activity on social media, the construction of self through the public profile, is a form of willing into existence the form of the big Other as those social networks that confer existence upon our contructed identities—identities that are no more concrete than those of Racheal or Deckard.

According to Slavoj Žižek,[29] this is experienced, ideologically, as a form of cynicism, which for him mirrors the psychoanalytic description of fetishism disavowal (the primary motor of perverse subjectivity): I know very well, but nevertheless …. Or, as Todd McGowan describes it, cynicism "is a mode of keeping alive the dream of successfully attaining the lost object [of desire], while fetishistically denying one's investment in this idea." Cynicism, he explains, "allows subjects to acknowledge the hopelessness of consumption while simultaneously consuming with as much hope as the most naïve consumer."[30] To put matters differently, today the postmodern subject is well aware of the problems that we continue to face: the looming threat of ecological catastrophe; deepening economic crises; increasing levels of personal/household and national/sovereign debt; further measures of austerity and the defunding of public and social services; war, terrorism, and the mass migration of those affected in the Middle East and northern Africa; not to mention rising forms of state violence toward racialized minorities, and new forms of racism, sexism, fundamentalism, as well as econonomic, social, and political apartheid. In the midst of all of this—where the problem is not one of false consciousness, we know, but nevertheless—ideology becomes operative through pratices of disavowal. And, it is here too that *Blade Runner*, as a work of dystopian fiction bridges toward the postmodern conception of cynicism, and one that prefigures capitalist realism.

Future imperfect; or, "it's easier to imagine the end of the world ..."

Blade Runner, therefore, brings to the foreground some of the basic insights of postmodern critical theory. It draws out a critique of modern ontology and ties together questions about the status of the subject and of reality. It puts to question our conception(s) of history, time, and memory, both in the story and in relation to the development of the characters, but also at the level of its form. The film is aesthetically postmodern for the way that it uses pastiche stylistically—it quotes and references past genres and styles. Where the new is no longer available, or possible, also where authenticity and originality are a thing of the past, only the resurrection of the past can produce the new. In this falling back on the past—quotations and references to the past—we find a central distinction between the modern and the postmodern. With modernism, the striving for the new—"make it new!"—gave it a Promethean character. The moderns strove to be original, authentic, and unique, but at the same time left destruction along its path. Modernism was based on grand visions of progress, but—as Adorno and Horkheimer argued—this "forward" movement of modernism resulted in some of the most oppressive logics. We see this in the history of twentieth-century Europe, with the rise of fascism and totalitarianism, for instance. It's not difficult to understand, then, the kind of cynicism that arises with postmodernism.

If modernism was about big utopian projects, then dystopia is the key motif of postmodernism. *Blade Runner* exemplifies postmodern cynicism perfectly. The world that it depicts, as we have seen, is one of postindustrial decay, where signs of late capitalism and remnants of the branded consumer culture abound. Power is held in the hands of a large corporation— the Tyrell Corporation; the world is dark and depressed. The world in this film is cruel and immoral. The multicultural slums seethe on the streets below, while the affluent cosmopolitans survive high above in the towering cybernetic pyramids.

One of the most interesting things about *Blade Runner* is that, on the one hand, it still prefigures not only elements of a later postmodern aesthetic but also the postmodern present, and, on the other hand, the closer we approach the time of *Blade Runner*—that is, the closer we get to the year 2019— its "future imperfect" still resonates. Though we are getting closer to being contemporaries of the diegetic time of the film, it still seems to portray for us the "future." Why does the future of *Blade Runner*—the dystopian future that it depicts—still resonate?

The 2007 Final Cut version of the film is said to be the last "rewriting" (so to speak) of the film. But one can well imagine yet another version of the film where the date is changed so that it still depicts for us a possible "future." That is to say that even in the various versions of the film we can historicize our postmodern times. Some of the chief differences in each version of the film mark different moments within the emergence and crystallization of the postmodern. The ending of the original US Theatrical Release, with its happy unification of the couple driving up north, escaping the city, clearly still holds onto a remainder of modern populism. The escape to nature is still utopian. With the Director's Cut and the scrapping of this ending, along with the voiceover narration and the added unicorn scene, Deckard's humanity is put into question. Here, in 1992, we are at the height of postmodernism. Not without significance, the Director's Cut was released at the same moment as the demise of the Soviet Union, the victory of liberal democracy, and the triumph of global capitalism. Francis Fukuyama's book *The End of History and the Last Man* was also published in the same year—a book that politically marks conservative postmodernism, and encapsulates particularly Margaret Thatcher's statement from nearly a decade prior, that "there is no alternative." "End of history"; "end of ideology"; "there is no alternative"—these are statements that highlight the cynicism of political postmodernism.

Mark Fisher uses the term "capitalist realism" to describe our current age—one that, according to him, has come after postmodernism. Postmodernism emerged at a moment when there was still conceivably an alternative to capitalism. It has now been more than three decades since the concept was originally theorized in cultural, social, and political theory. Today, no viable alternatives to capitalism seem to really exist. Fisher defines "capitalist realism" by referring to the statement often attributed to Jameson and Žižek, that it is easier to imagine the end of the world than the end of capitalism.[31] This statement works materially as well as ideologically.

Postmodernism, according to Marxists like Jameson and Žižek, is the cultural logic of late capitalism, which we might also view in relation to the rise of neoliberalism and the dominance of finance capital. It is in terms of finance capital that we can even go further in understanding the logic behind the "breakdown of the signifying chain," or the "demise of symbolic efficiency," or even the concept of the postmodern "perpetual present." Deleuze and Guattari are correct in linking the deconstruction of meaning in late capitalism to the market imperative to transcend barriers that might prohibit or limit exchange in the interest of procuring more profit. Finance capital pushes this even further, particularly mixed with the political logic of neoliberalism, which has as part of its objective the dismantling of state mechanisms that limited possibilities of trade and exchange of financial commodities. With finance capital, it is much truer that "all that is solid melts into air." But also, what is finance if not a mechanism for borrowing from the future? Finance means that we borrow from our own future (earnings) in order to pay for things in the present. In this way, the future never seems to arise because it has already been borrowed. We end up constantly working toward paying back what we borrowed from our future selves. In this way, we are constantly living in a perpetual present.[32] *Blade Runner*, in its various different versions, seems to encapsulate this fact of a constant perpetual present in cultural form.

With each new stage in postmodernity, from its post-Keynesian beginning to the "end of history" period, and even today in capitalist realism, the film has received new treatment, marking the historical moment in some way. It is postmodern simulation and simulacra of itself. Every version is a copy without an original. As I discussed at the beginning of this chapter, it is increasingly difficult to discern which version is the true original. Like *Star Wars*, *Blade Runner* never seems to be complete. In this way, then, the film provides a kind of "cognitive mapping" for the postmodern present. What does it mean when someone says "I've seen *Blade Runner*"? Which *Blade Runner*? The film as a referent to itself is lost. With the announcement of the release of a sequel to the film directed by Denis Villeneuve in 2017, we might well ask the question: sequel to which *Blade Runner*? How will this new film mark the previous versions of the film? How will this film retroactively re-create *Blade Runner*? History, it would still seem, is never final; it is neither complete, nor unique. There may be multiple histories (plural), but it is important to remember that the past is sutured by the politics and culture of the present, which itself is defined by visions of the possible future. As a critical dystopia, *Blade Runner* can still define the capitalist realism of our present. It is a dialectical image that, on the one hand, provides insights into conceptions of the subject, but on the other hand, it is (still) a look ahead into the negative aspects of unfettered multinational capitalism.

Notes

1 "Star Wars Special Edition Changes HD." *Google+* Web. Viewed January 6, 2016.

2 *Blade Runner*'s status as "postmodern" has been debated by theorists such as Scott Bukatman and Kaja Silverman, who both claim that the film is rather an example of high or late modernism, while others, like Guiliana Bruno and David Harvey, claim that it is unquestionably postmodern. Others like Vivian Sobchack take a more moderate view, proposing that *Blade Runner* treads the line between high-modernism and postmodernism. See Scott Bukatman, *Blade Runner* 2nd ed. (London: BFI and Palgrave Macmillan, 2012); Kaja Silverman, "Back to the Future." *Camera Obscura* 9.3 27 (1991): 109–32; Guiliana Bruno, "Ramble City: Postmodernism and *Blade Runner*." *October* 41 (1987): 61–74; David Harvey, *The Condition of Postmodernity* (Oxford: Blackwell, 1990); Vivian Sobchack, *Screening Space: The American Science Fiction Film*, 2nd enlarged ed. (New York: Ungar, 1987), 272.

3 For detailed discussions of the production background to the various versions of the film, see Paul M. Sammon, *Future Noir: The Making of Blade Runner* (New York: Harper Collins, 1996); and Kenneth Turan, "Behind the Scenes: *Blade Runner*." In *Now in Theatres Everywhere: A Celebration of a Certain Kind of Blockbuster* (New York: Public Affairs, 2006).

4 See Lev Manovich, *The Language of New Media* (Cambridge, MA: MIT Press, 2001), 302.

5 I'm drawing, here, on a point that Fisher makes regarding the infinite "plasticity," reality, and instability of capitalism in capitalist realism. Mark Fisher, *Capitalist Realism: Is There No Alternative?* (Winchester, UK: Zero Books, 2009), 54.

6 Fredric Jameson, "Postmodernism and Consumer Society." In
   *The Cultural Turn: Selected Writings on the Postmodern, 1983–
   1998* (New York: Verso, 1998), 10.

7 Here, for the sake of brevity, I have chosen not to consider the
   sequels to *Back to the Future*, in which the characters do, in
   fact, travel to the future.

8 Silverman, "Back to the Future," 109.

9 See Scott Bukatman, *Terminal Identity: The Virtual Subject in
   Postmodern Science Fiction* (Durham, NC: Duke University
   Press, 1993), 103–56.

10 Bukatman (1993 and 2012) provides a good general overview of
   the aesthetic inspiration for *Blade Runner*'s set design.

11 See Benjamin, "The Work of Art in the Age of Mechanical
   Reproduction." In *Illuminations: Essays and Reflections*.
   Trans. Hannah Arendt (New York: Schocken, 1969); George
   Simmel, "The Metropolis and Mental Life." In *The Blackwell
   City Reader*, ed. Gary Bridge and Sophie Watson (Malden,
   MA: Wiley-Blackwell, 2002). See also Susan Buck-Morss,
   "Aesthetics and Anaesthetics: Walter Benjamin's Artwork Essay
   Reconsidered." *October* 62: 3–41, 1992.

12 David Harvey, *The Condition of Postmodernity*
   (Oxford: Blackwell, 1990), 311.

13 Jameson, "Postmodernism, or, the Cultural Logic of Late
   Capitalism," 53–92, 83.

14 Bukatman, *Blade Runner*, 55.

15 This metaphorical and visual distinction between the spaces of
   the slums and the spaces of the elite are also a mirror reflection
   of some of the consumer spaces that populate the world today,
   such as the total spaces of shopping malls and department
   stores, like Toronto's Eaton Centre, which Jameson describes
   as a kind of miniature city, but which should be noted for the
   way that its spatial design allots lower-end stores to the bottom
   floor and basement, and higher-end stores up above on the
   upper floors. See Jameson, "Postmodernism and Consumer
   Society," 12.

16 The Esper machine is replicated on the menu screens of the
   DVD and Blu-ray releases of the Final Cut version of the film.

17 N. Katherine Hayles, *How We Became Posthuman: Virtual
   Bodies in Cybernetics, Literature, and Informatics*
   (Chicago: University of Chicago Press, 1999), 161–2.

18 Jameson, "Postmodernism, or, the Cultural Logic of Late
    Capitalism," 53–92, 72.
19 For a more detailed discussion of this scene see Matthew
    Flisfeder, *The Symbolic, The Sublime, and Slavoj Žižek's
    Theory of Film* (New York: Palgrave Macmillan, 2012),
    151–8.
20 For more on this argument, see Mathias Nilges, "The Anti-Anti-
    Oedipus: Representing Post-Fordist Subjectivity." *Mediations*
    23(2): 26–69, 2008.
21 Mark Fisher, *Capitalist Realism*, 58.
22 Foucault, "Nietzsche, Genealogy, History." In *The Foucault
    Reader*, edited by Paul Rabinow (New York: Pantheon, 1984).
23 Silverman, "Back to the Future," 119.
24 Foucault, cited in Bruno, "Ramble City," 72.
25 Slavoj Žižek, *Tarrying with the Negative: Kant, Hegel, and the
    Critique of Ideology* (Durham, NC: Duke University Press,
    1993), 10. The question of "class consciousness" is for Žižek
    also tied to the phenomenon of consciousness as such. In *Blade
    Runner*, he points out that the question of self-consciousness
    is even posited in the homophone between "Deckard" and
    "Descartes."
26 See Jameson, *The Political Unconscious: Narrative as a Socially
    Symbolic Act* (Ithaca, NY: Cornell University Press, 1981).
27 Manovich, *The Language of New Media*, 226
28 On this topic, see Matthew Flisfeder, "Enjoying Social Media,"
    in *Žižek and Media Studies: A Reader*, eds. Matthew Flisfeder
    and Louis-Paul Willis (New York: Palgrave Macmillan,
    2014); and Flisfeder, "The Entrepreneurial Subject and the
    Objectivization of the Self in Social Media." *South Atlantic
    Quarterly* 114.3 (2015): 553–70.
29 See in particular Slavoj Žižek, *The Sublime Object of Ideology*
    (New York: Verso, 1989); and *The Ticklish Subject.*
30 Todd McGowan, *Out of Time: Desire in Atemporal Cinema*
    (Minneapolis: University of Minnesota Press, 2011), 29.
31 Fisher, *Capitalist Realism*; Fredric Jameson, *The Seeds of Time*
    (New York: Columbia University Press, 1994); Slavoj Žižek,
    "The Spectre of Ideology." In *Mapping Ideology*, ed. Slavoj
    Žižek (New York: Verso, 1994).
32 On this point, see Matthew Flisfeder, "Communism and the End
    of the World." *Public* 48: 105–15, 2013.

Conclusion

Postmodern theory after the end of history

Postmodernism is a theory of culture that begins first as a reaction to modern narratives of history, including liberal and Enlightenment narratives of progress, and dialectical models of change and transformation, particularly Marxist historical materialism. As we have seen, the postmodern incredulity toward grand narratives has also been met on the Right by theories of the "end of history." The end of the Cold War and the apparent victories of liberal democracy and the capitalist "market" economy demonstrated for those on the Right that the big narratives of history had come to an end. The world has finally settled on *the* model; now all that we have to do, supposedly, is to integrate everyone into the one big model. Also, with the demise of the Soviet Union and European Communism, big ideological disputes no longer resonate— there is no longer a dispute between which political and economic systems are better; now that capitalism has won, all that is left is the pragmatic, neutral administration of the world. Postmodernism, which was sewn mainly in the postwar period could then, in the 1990s, flourish as a cultural dominant, when big questions about revolution and social transformation slowly shifted into small questions about identity. Class war transformed into culture war.

It is hard not to discern in postmodernism a certain variety of cynical logic that has shied away from big emancipatory projects. Nevertheless, we would be remiss to suggest that postmodernism has not brought with it significant critical categories that have potentially furthered the project of emancipation. Contemporary politics have been enhanced, rather than harmed, by two decades' worth of proliferating identity politics. Identity politics and cultural studies have helped to fill in some significant gaps in Left politics. Nevertheless, the problem with identity politics is that there is nothing inherently radical about them. Identity, like culture, is perfectly commodifiable, and diffusible into the mainstream of capitalist society. As Jameson has recently put it, postmodernism is "the very name for the hegemony of the commodity as it perpetuates itself in the form of a thoroughgoing and inescapable aestheticization of daily life."[1] As the commodity has taken precedence over daily life, it has become increasingly difficult to discern any concrete figure antagonistic to the project of emancipation. Under the reign of the commodity, even the bourgeoisie as a primarily cultural (as opposed to economic) category has lost its clout. Even the Right, today, is largely antibourgeois, preferring to combine populist rhetoric with the uninhibited logic of the market (figures like Donald Trump and Sarah Palin, and the former mayor of Toronto, Rob Ford, are exemplary here). At least the liberal bourgeoisie still placed high regard on values of equality and democracy. The problem with the bourgeoisie was that it found itself incapable of recognizing the fact that equality remains impossible within the logic of capital. Our situation today presents us with the paradox of a class struggle on the Right, where the latter appears to be more capable of interpellating the working class, by presenting the postmodern Left—tied rhetorically to the validation of political correctness—as the ruling class.

Postmodernism is the result of a loss of the Symbolic in the form of practices of interpretation, specifically dialectical theories of history found in Marx and Hegel, and psychoanalysis. The loss of the Symbolic has meant the loss of "depth models," such as the dynamic between essence and appearance, base and superstructure, authenticity and inauthenticity, signifier and signified, and the psychoanalytic model of repression. This loss, we have seen, is what figures like Lyotard, Foucault, and Deleuze and Guattari find not only favorable but also necessarily tied to practices of contemporary critique. For Lyotard, the coming of postindustrial society shifted historical gears from the economic to the technological. Instead of emancipation, the shift in the mode of production brought more domination, hence invalidating the Marxist theory of historical progression. Foucault's insights and criticism of the dialectical method, inspired by Nietzsche and his genealogical approach allow us to see in liberal and Marxist histories an underlying subjective perspective, potentially tied to the authority of power–knowledge—in which later feminist and postcolonial theorists have found a particularly masculine and Western bias—that seems to undermine the logic of emancipation. Deleuze and Guattari, likewise, see in psychoanalysis a territorializing practice that returns the subject to the oppressive logic of the patriarchal, conjugal bourgeois family. If with these thinkers we find a loss of the liberatory impact of critical interpretation, then Jameson's use of the "breakdown" metaphor is quite apt. Losing the categories of history and subjectivity as models of critical interpretation, it is almost as if critical theory has suffered from a loss of the Symbolic—the Symbolic, that is, as a practice of interpretation that allows the subject to locate herself in the context of her exploitation and/or oppression. This, I would argue, is the problem today with populist right-wing rhetoric. Lacking critical practices of interpretation—lacking because they have been discredited by both the Right *and* the postmodern Left—the Right now is better positioned to win at the hegemony game. Perhaps, with the rise of capitalist realism—and the "end of history"—it is time for (capital 'H') History to get back on its steady march forward.

It's in the politics of the 1960s that we also see this first shift away from class struggle and into the various identity politics. During the period of the rising social welfare state, a period of class compromise between capital and labor, where capital agreed to sacrifice short-term profits in return for the long-term stability of the system, we saw the proliferation of non-class based political movements, from the rise of new postcolonial nationalist movements internationally, and the rise of the civil rights movement in the United States, second wave feminism in North America and Europe, the antiwar movement, the students' movement, and the gay liberation movement. As these movements slowly penetrated the mainstream, and made their way into the humanities and social science departments of the universities, their effects could be found in changes to the curriculum, where new forms of critical theory challenged the traditional and elitist brands of scholarship. Cultural studies provided a model for the new integration of postcolonial, non-white, and feminist literature into the academy, and later, in the 1990s, Queer Theory finally broke through the heteronormativity of the academy. Although identity politics started to gain support above modern class politics, its subversive potential is somewhat diminished by consumer society, which has managed to open a space for its diffusion.

We can understand postmodernism as tied to the rise of the postwar consumer society, again, with the rising social welfare state, as people were increasingly able to enjoy the benefits of mass consumption. In consumer society, there is very little space for the non-commodifiable. In postmodern consumer society, the hegemony of the commodity comes out in full force, where it begins to look like there is nothing that is not commodity. In this sense, art and mass culture start to blend into each other. Whereas in modernism, art held strongly to its vocation to not become commodity—that is, modern art emerged as those forms and styles that endeavoured to avoid falling into commodification and mass culture—postmodern art is what we got when that attempt to evade commodification was no longer fully possible. Likewise, the subversive edge of identity politics begins to lose sway when we start to witness the various ways that identity becomes just more content for advertising and marketing. Consumer society, and consumer culture, seems to allow everyone to "be who they want to be." Modern culture, which still found itself bound by older ideals and traditions, older forms of patriarchal authority, appeared to place a limitation on identity, plotting people into traditional binary positions and codes. Postmodernism and consumer society provides a space for people to experience a kind of freedom from that older authority. In consumer society, it looks like we are nowhere prohibited from enjoying, but increasingly we are pushed toward obligated enjoyment. The overarching commandment of postmodern society is not "Stop enjoying!" It is instead, "Why aren't you enjoying yet?" Authority seems to have disappeared—an authority that said "No!" The apparent victory of liberal democracy, following the Cold War, also seems to have evaporated authority—now we are all supposedly free (to consume). This, too, is the logical result of the final institutionalization of modernism, which took subversion as its primary goal. What becomes of subversion (of authority), when subversion itself becomes the official and institutionalized practice of art and culture?[2]

Postmodernism emerges, then, not when modernism disappears, but when it becomes everything and is found everywhere—that is, paradoxically, when modernism itself becomes the dominant ideology, but only to the extent that it permits a more total colonization of the commodity—so, it is subversion minus subversion; or, in other words, it is the *appearance* of subversion. In the postmodern society of the spectacle, appearance matters more than essence, and in this primacy given to the surficial, those ideals to which modernism found itself devoted, such as depth, originality, and novelty, seem to perish. The punk rock politics of "anarchy in the UK," descends into a mere fashion decision. Body piercings and tattoos become "body art." Surfaces seem to matter more than depth.

Postmodernism is also a product of new regimes of representation and simulation. Beyond the society of the spectacle we find an atmosphere of the hyperreal, where the model—the representation—*precedes* the real thing. The hyperreal allows us to rethink the relationship between representation and ideology. In an older view, representation had to do with a false portrayal of reality. There was reality—the real reality—and then there was a representation. In analyzing the representation, all that was required was examining the variance between the representation and the reality. The concept of the hyperreal diminishes this depth model of a deeper reality, and proposes that there is no reality—no *meaningful* reality, that is—apart or outside of the representation. This is not merely to suggest that reality exists only in representation, but it does highlight the fact that *meaning* only comes to us *as* represented. Therefore, it is not a matter of having false representations of reality—which an older ideology critique might try to argue. The postmodern critique of representation shows that not only ideology, but all history, and the meanings tied to both, are a matter of representation—mediated representations that *precede* the real. To make matters more concrete, we might then say that what postmodern critical theory tries to highlight is that media is not in the business of producing a *false* consciousness, it tries to show that all consciousness, all meaning, comes to us *as* mediated or *pre*-mediated.

The bleeding together of art and commodity also has meant a transcendence of class lines in postmodern culture, where the commodity itself becomes art, just as art is further commodified. I have already used the example of Warhol's soup cans, but this example is effective in showing how postmodernism takes objects of the everyday culture of the population—a culture that *is* highly commodified because of consumer society—and raises these objects to the level of art. This is not a mere celebration of the commodity as art, it is rather the fact of turning the everyday lifeworld of popular culture into art, and it is just a matter of fact that popular culture is commodified culture. So postmodernism treads a line between the populism of the everyday lifeworld of the people, and the fact of popular culture existing as a commodified consumer culture. The Campbell's soup can is art, not because it is commodity but because it is a product of the everyday. The same can be said about a film like *Blade Runner*. We can treat it as art, and read it this way, despite the fact that it is a product of mass consumer culture. It is, in this way, doubly coded.

Returning, then, to questions about history, we can also conclude that postmodernism is something like the dialectics of history at a standstill. If modernism was partly defined by the ethic to "make it new," postmodernism is what happens when the new seems to have run out of steam. There is no longer any room for development. No longer anything to diffuse into the commodity, since the commodity has now colonized all space so completely. When everything is commodity, the vocation to not be commodity becomes near to impossible. On one side, then, postmodern style is merely a recycled, de-historicized reference to modern styles and genres, in the form of pastiche. Though, as critics like Hutcheon try to show, postmodernism, while referencing past styles and genres, parodies them in order to put them under a critical microscope. Is *Blade Runner* doubly coded in this way? It is both commodity-spectacle *and* an aesthetic masterpiece.

We have seen that *Blade Runner* exemplifies postmodern pastiche in its combination of sci-fi and film noir. Its sci-fi conventions include the fact that it is set in the future, the plot pays attention to technology and science, and the setting is characterized by high tech environments. But its plot also references qualities of an older film noir. Rachael portrays the typical femme fatale, Deckard simulates the hardboiled detective. The portrayal and mise-en-scène are dark, and the atmosphere is dreary. Deckard's narration in the original US Theatrical Release is also a stereotype of past noir styles. The film then is definitely representative of what Jameson has called the "nostalgia mode" of postmodernism. It represents, not the past styles or genres directly, but stereotypes of past styles. Though set in the future, *Blade Runner*, like *Star Wars*, represents stereotypes of the past sci-fi serial; it represents a stereotype of the noir film and noir conventions. Nevertheless, despite this combination of past and future, *Blade Runner* is undoubtedly a film about the postmodern present. We see this particularly in its attention to the branded, retrofitted environment of the cybernetic city.

Blade Runner's attention to technology, technological environments, simulation, and the hyperreal, moves it beyond a mere reference to past styles. It puts into question modern conceptions of subjectivity, and still reflects the multinational dynamics of late capitalism. The look of the film is glossed with references to the cybernetic, and has become, along with films like *Tron* and *Videodrome*, one of the progenitors of the cyberpunk genre in film, later emulated by films like *The Matrix*, *Johnny Mnemonic*, *Strange Days*, and *Robocop*. *Blade Runner*, like these other films, puts corporate power in the hot seat, making of it the villain, while its layout—the layout of the city, that is—reflects the rhizomatic networks of multinational capitalism. In the film, the replicants are constructed, not all together at some big warehouse at the Tyrell Corporation. They are manufactured in parts—some here, some there—by Chew in his laboratory, by Sebastian at the hollowed-out Bradbury building. Like the story of the Nike sneaker in the networks of global capitalism, the NEXUS 6 replicants are manufactured like any other commodity. They are themselves commodities, but are they not also slaves? This last point puts not only *their* "humanity," but also *our own* into question.

In the original US Theatrical Release, it is Rachael who acts a kind of mediator. She exists between the replicants and the humans in the film. She is a replicant, but she experiences herself as human. This is so because she has had artificial memories implanted into her brain. She also possesses concrete evidence of her past—of her history—in the form of the photograph of her with her mother, which she later discovers is actually a photograph of Tyrell's niece. In the Director's Cut, Deckard's humanity is also put into question. The origami unicorn left by Gaff at the end indicates that Deckard's daydream of the unicorn was implanted as well. Deckard is a replicant. But what does that tell us about our own conception of subjectivity?

Postmodernism questions the modern conception of the liberal human subject—the centered conception of the Self. On two levels: at the level of our conscious awareness of ourselves, and at the level of the human body. The more we see how our bodies are machine-like, or tied to machines for our very survival, and how our subjective sense of Self is a matter of ideology and of representation, the more we can come to question the modern sense of the subject that we have assumed. Putting memory and history into question—showing that history and memory are a matter of objectivization, reified in the form of media and storage hardware—troubles the sense of depth that we hold onto when we conceptualize the individual human subject.

Blade Runner attends to questions of race and class, too, in interesting ways. Though they are all white, the replicants are still racialized in a way. They are singled out, excluded, for unequal treatment and exploitation because of the type of body that they have. They are seen as less than human and therefore their exploitation on the Off-World colonies is justified. At the same time, the city is itself racialized. Space plays an important role in this depiction. The elite—Tyrell, the police headquarters—exist literally above everyone else in the film. Below are the decayed slums of the city, populated by an orientalized mass.

Blade Runner therefore exemplifies postmodernism and postmodern critical theory by attending to the major points of criticism discussed in Chapter One: master narratives, cultural and media representation, Eurocentrism/phallocentrism, and the liberal-Cartesian conception of the subject. It deals with questions of master narrative and History strategically, questioning an objective, neutral understanding of history by playing with themes of memory and retroactivity in the replicants themselves. It even troubles the Oedipalization of human subjects by attending to the relationship between the replicants and the mother/father dynamic: Leon is asked about his mother at the beginning of the film, Rachael is implanted with a memory of her mother, Tyrell is portrayed as a father figure for Roy. Tyrell embodies the figure of authority against which the replicants rebel. Style, genre, pastiche, parody, irony are all dealt with in the way that the film represents the story. Internal to the film, depth and flatness are played with as well when Deckard uses the Esper machine to investigate Leon's photograph. The Esper machine plays on the theme of flatness and depth. The image that Deckard searches through is pure two-dimensional surface, but it still manages to become three-dimensional in the way that it is navigated, almost as if it was a space of virtual reality. Subjectivity, finally, is seen to be technologically mediated, first in terms of the technological bodies of the replicants, and second with the use of technology to transcend the limitations of the human body. Both the Esper machine and the Voight-Kampff test extend the human eye, showing that there is never a human *essence* that is deeper than the surface level of techno-/post-human.

However, what remains striking about *Blade Runner* is that, despite the fact that we are quickly approaching the year 2019, the year in which the film takes place, its depiction of the "future" still resonates. The future of *Blade Runner* still looks like *our* potential future. It is a dystopia that still carries an impact for our capitalist present. As discussed at the end of the last chapter, *Blade Runner*, like other films and novels about dystopia and postapocalyptic societies, mirrors the statement attributed to Jameson and Žižek, that it is easier to imagine the end of the world than the end of capitalism. This statement, more than any other, expresses postmodern cynicism at its core. But it increasingly makes sense when we consider the cultural logic of finance capital. What is finance if not the need to borrow from the future (future earnings, the potential of future profit) in order to pay for the present? When we do this, we continuously rob ourselves of our own future, and we end up living in a perpetual present. *Blade Runner* is at the same time a reflection—a representation—of our postmodern present, *and* a critical extrapolation of the future of capitalist realism. Read allegorically, *Blade Runner* expresses for us many of the themes that we have already explored—themes expressive of the postmodern. But more than that, the reading of the film provided here shows how, methodologically, an intertextual interpretation of cinema, popular culture, and media generally, provides the kind of cognitive mapping of our current predicaments that the modern compartmentalization and fragmentation of knowledge—the kind that Habermas described, and which was dealt with at the beginning of Chapter One—made even more difficult. In this way, the postmodern reading of culture and popular culture can accomplish what the modern Enlightenment aspired toward, but failed to do because of the authority vested in the cannon and the expert. Postmodern criticism can bring together theory and popular culture in a way that was too often dismissed by modern art and criticism. So where does this leave us?

If, by the 1990s, postmodernism had become a cultural dominant, what then are we to make of our current era? As I noted at the beginning of this book, postmodernism is a conception of culture that has been on the wane since the turn of the century. Two events in the first decade of the twenty-first century—the attacks on the World Trade Center on September 11, 2001, and the financial crisis that began with the 2007–2008 subprime mortgage crisis in the United States—seem to indicate that something new *has* emerged: what Fisher calls "capitalist realism." With capitalist realism, it appears as though there is no longer any alternative to global capitalism. The cynicism of postmodernism and its incredulity toward grand narratives has potentially rid us of all of the twentieth-century conceptions of alternatives to capitalism. But the last few years have shown signs that perhaps History has once again started to move forward. Since 2011 we have seen a whole array of new political mobilizations and uprisings. From the so-called Arab Spring, to Occupy Wall Street, and renewed interest in Socialism and neo-Communism,[3] it would seem that class struggle and grand narrative are once again becoming popular, particularly with younger generations. The rebooting of *Blade Runner*, first with the Final Cut, and now with the sequel set to be released in 2017, is perhaps significant in this regard. Postmodern dystopian fiction, in other films, like Alfonso Cuarón's *Children of Men*, provides for us a kind of cognitive mapping of our potential future, should things continue unchanged. *Blade Runner* still looks like the potential future of capitalist realism, which is why it still impresses upon us. But the closer we get to the year 2019, in which the film is set, the sooner it will become necessary to imagine a real historical alternative.

Notes

1 Fredric Jameson, "Gherman's Anti-Aesthetic." *New Left Review* 97 (2016): 95–105, 96.
2 Or, as Slavoj Žižek puts it, when perversion is no longer subversion. See *The Ticklish Subject*, 247–312. Perry Anderson also notes that "Modernism, from its earliest origins in Baudelaire or Flaubert onwards, virtually defined itself as 'anti-bourgeois.' Postmodernism is what occurs when, without any victory, that adversary is gone." *The Origins of Postmodernity* (New York: Verso, 1998), 86. Terry Eagleton, likewise, argues that postmodernism is the result of a perceived failure of the Left in the post-1968 period, a failure he suggests that never actually took place. Terry Eagleton, *The Illusions of Postmodernism* (Malden, MA: Blackwell, 1996).
3 See for instance Alain Badiou, *The Communist Hypothesis* (New York: Verso, 2008); Bruno Bosteels, *The Actuality of Communism* (New York: Verso, 2011); Jodi Dean, *The Communist Horizon* (New York: Verso, 2012); and Slavoj Žižek, *First as Tragedy, Then as Farce* (New York: Verso, 2009).

FURTHER READING

Benedict Anderson, *The Origins of Postmodernity* (New York: Verso, 1998).

Anderson's book should be read as a companion piece to Fredric Jameson's study of postmodernism as the cultural logic of late capitalism. The book provides a historical overview of the emergence of postmodernism and postmodernity, and develops some important insights on Jameson's theory of postmodernism.

Marshall Berman, *All That Is Solid Melts into Air: The Experience of Modernity* (New York: Penguin, 1982).

In this book, Berman develops a dialectical interpretation for the emergence of modernism, modernity, and modernization. He traces this emergence through in-depth analyses of Goethe's *Faust*, the *Communist Manifesto*, the poetry of Charles Baudelaire, modern architecture in New York City, and the processes of modernization in Eastern Europe.

Stephen Best and Douglas Kellner, *The Postmodern Turn* (New York: Guilford Press, 1997).

This text is useful for introducing readers to the many different areas in which postmodernism has had an influence, including philosophy, cultural theory, and science. The book also provides a clear overview of some of the key theorists tied to postmodern theory.

Terry Eagleton, *The Illusions of Postmodernism* (Malden, MA: Blackwell, 1996).

Eagleton's book is useful as a Marxist critique of postmodernism. Eagleton assesses the emergence of postmodernism as a perceived failure of the Left. The writing is lucid and clear, and helpful for introducing an alternative take to familiar themes in postmodern theory.

Mark Fisher, *Capitalist Realism: Is There No Alternative?* (Winchester, UK: Zero Books, 2009).

In this short text, Mark Fisher looks at some of the cultural developments that have taken place in the period following postmodernism. Drawing on arguments made by Fredric Jameson, Slavoj Žižek, and Gilles Deleuze, Fisher proposes the concept of "capitalist realism" to describe the contemporary form of cynical ideology.

Hal Foster, ed., *The Anti-Aesthetic: Essays on Postmodern Culture* (New York: New Press, 1998).

The essays in this anthology are some of the first major works to define and develop the key theses on postmodern visual and cultural theory. Its approaches combine critical and cultural theory with art history and criticism.

David Harvey, *The Condition of Postmodernity* (Oxford: Blackwell, 1989).

In this book, Harvey develops a political economic analysis for the emergence of postmodernism and postmodernity, showing how its emergence is tied to transformations in global capitalism from Fordism to post-Fordism, and in this way the work serves as a counterpart to Jameson's cultural analysis of postmodernism, which shows the underlying political economic forces of contemporary postmodern culture.

Linda Hutcheon, *The Politics of Postmodernism*, 2nd ed. (New York: Routledge, 2002).

Hutcheon's text posits a politics of postmodernism grounded firmly in postmodern theory. Her argument contrasts with the Marxist arguments of Jameson, but clearly shows the usefulness and significance of postmodern criticism and its practices of interrogation.

Fredric Jameson, *Postmodernism, or, The Cultural Logic of Late Capitalism* (Durham, NC: Duke University Press, 1990).

This book is a seminal text in the critical analysis of postmodernism. Jameson develops a historical materialist analysis of postmodern culture and provides a detailed discussion of the elementary components of postmodernism.

Jean-François Lyotard, *The Postmodern Condition: A Report on Knowledge.* Translated by Geoff Bennington and Brian Massumi (Minneapolis: University of Minnesota Press, 1984).

Lyotard's study provides the first clear definition of postmodernism, as an incredulity toward metanarratives, and is therefore a good starting point for the continued study and interrogation of postmodernism. It can be seen, along with Jameson's *Postmodernism*, as essential reading for beginning to understand the debates in postmodern theory.

INDEX